The D₁Evolution Of M

by Clive Gregory
with cartoons and illustrations by Calvin Beedle

Edited by: Alison Gregory

Illustrations and Cartoons: Calvin Beedle

Photos: R & C Gregory Publishing Limited

Cover design by: Calvin Beedle and Clive Gregory

The seeds of this project were sown while writing the first music tutor books for R & C Gregory Publishing Ltd. The 'about the band' sketches were an immediate hit with music students. I would like to acknowledge the ideas and support of Geoff Ellwood (author of "Everything You Need To Know About Being A Keyboard Player") who played a significant part as editor and author of many of those early sketches. This book was written by Clive Gregory in the spring of 2001. The project really took shape once Calvin Beedle was signed as illustrator and we'd like to acknowledge his talent and enthusiasm in developing the project - wait for it - on time. A first for R & C.

Thanks to:
Peter Wall, Rubiah Gregory, Geoff Ellwood,
Noeleen Beedle, Calvin Beedle, Andrew Newbold and all
the gang at Colourscope and Croydon Reprographic.

Published by
R & C Gregory Publishing Limited
Suite 7, Unit 6, Beckenham Business Centre, Cricket Lane, Kent.   BR3 1LB
www.psst.co.uk/devolution

R. & C. GREGORY
PUBLISHING LIMITED

ISBN 1-901690-50-4

Printed in the United Kingdom by C.S. PRINT & DISPLAY LIMITED. Croydon, England.

The Devolution Of Musicians

by *Clive Gregory*
with cartoons and illustrations by *Calvin Beedle*

All the characters in this book are the creation of the author and illustrator.

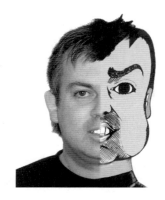

Clive Gregory - author
Basso complex onceuponatimeus

Author of "Learn Bass From Beginner To Your 1st Band", "A Great Way To Learn Bass" and "Clive Gregory's Foundation Course For Bass Guitar". About time he wrote something not about the Bass Guitar then. This is his first fictional work and is definitely not based on any real people.

As always, dedicated to my wife, Rosiah.

Thanks to all the family Ta

Calvin Beedle - illustrator
Basso complex inhisparetimus

When looking for an illustrator we could think of no better qualification than a highly qualified picture framer - a member of the guild of picture framers no less. We also needed an artist who was a musician, who'd understand the need to classify this species. Calvin fitted our requirements perfectly.

To my fantastic wife Noeleen.

CONTENTS

INTRODUCTION TO THE EVOLUTION OF MUSICIANS

In the early spring of 1992, I was watching a band play at a London venue. The band was terrible, showcasing for a major record label. The audience was 90% musicians trying to see what all the hype was about. Seeing hundreds of musicians gathered together, mixing with a few ordinary people, it became obvious that musicians were only very distantly related to human beings. It was at this moment that I decided to make it my life's work to investigate the origin of the musician species. I was totally convinced that musicians had evolved in a totally different way and were a completely different species from the rest of mankind.

As my early investigations progressed, it became clear that not only did musicians evolve in a different way to humans but that within the family of musicians, there were many sub-species that had, in their own way, evolved into totally different species.

It was going to be imperative that the species be classified thoroughly if science was to unravel the mystery of their evolution.

Musicians have co-existed with man for all time but have very slowly evolved in different directions from man.

My studies quickly established that there were two distinct groups that split from *Homo sapiens*. I've called these groups *Homo musica* and *Homo submusica*. *Homo musica* are the genuine musician species, with natural instincts to make melody or harmony. *Homo submusica* developed alongside *Homo musica*, feeding off their creativity and either becoming sub-ordinate individuals attached to groups of *Homo musica*, such as *Drummus* and *Vocalis* or parasitic creatures like *Hangersonus*.

The distinction between *Homo musica* and *Homo submusica* is not immediately obvious to the layman. This is because it is largely neurological, so that without studying the brain and anatomy of the *submusica* species, we still wouldn't fully understand their stupidity. *Musica*, like *sapiens*, is intelligent and creative - *submusica* is more closely related to primates and reptiles - in that the brain is much smaller and the cerebral cortex in particular, is almost non-existent. *Submusica* can function within society but the finer, more subtle aspects of music must be left to the true *musica* species.

What I have endeavoured to do, over these past, long years, is for the first time, to classify each instrumental group or family of musicians.

The first step was to establish whether a group was *musica* or *submusica*. As this involved the dissection of each species it was a lengthy, possibly illegal operation and so had to be conducted in total secrecy. Altogether this took me nearly five years to complete and involved over 80 creatures. The second step was somewhat easier, although I was required to visit most countries of the world and log the activities of over 7000 *musica* and *submusica* from around the globe. On the next page is a chart that lists all currently discovered and classified species. Clearly there are still many species in the wild that have not yet been discovered and classified.

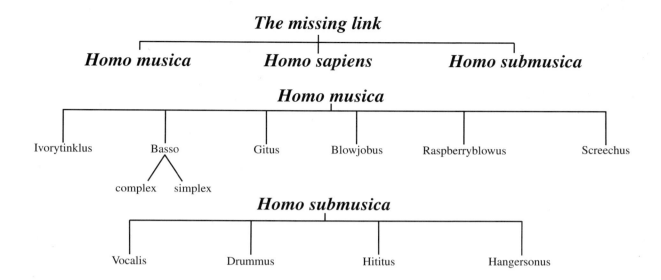

This book is first and foremost a study of Musicians. For the first time this strange species has been classified into scientific groups. The book is also intended to help the layman easily identify the precise group and species their musician of interest belongs to.

Don't expect to easily identify all species when they are wandering around the street. Some, such as *Vocalis grand prattus eyebrowsus*, are fairly easy to spot in any situation but most will require study in order to identify the precise species out of a musical environment.

So the novice musician spotter needs to begin in the club or concert hall. Keep this book with you at all times. When you see which instrument your target picks up you can obviously work out the family. At this point, look at the target and read the opening section describing the family. Keeping your target in vision, check each of the visual points and remember

them, as this will quickly enable you to spot each group, whether they are playing their instrument or not.

The precise species is in many ways easy to spot once you have established the instrumental family.

One complication in identification can occur when an instrumentalist also sings lead vocal. Vocalis species also sometimes try to use an instrument - usually because they can't move very well and need something to hide behind. So this is the clue. Vocalis don't actually play more than a few simple chords or melodies - the instrument being more or less decorative. Instrumentalists, on the other hand, will play their instrument completely throughout a show, singing as well as playing.

Happy hunting, I hope this book helps you understand more about this fascinating species.

ORIGIN

Vocalis are not believed to originate from any specific part of the globe. Rather they are a by-product of in-breeding amongst small groups like actors and media people. This in-breeding creates a serious mutation in over 95% of the resulting offspring and takes the form of excessive petulance, vanity and an urge to either undress or overdress at every opportunity.

It may be difficult at first to comprehend, but just because a person is classified a vocalist doesn't mean they can actually sing - the scientific classification is based solely on whether they are a 100% prat.

SIZE and GENERAL ANATOMY

Generally much smaller than they look on TV and in photos *vocalis* are usually they smallest of *Homo submusica*.

Anatomically, *vocalis* always have a dramatic natural feature, in males this can be oversized genitals or eyebrows. The females of the species may have excessive chest measurements or eyes. In extreme cases the two may be of identical size. Many females of the species may, in the early part of their career, develop the distinctive 'Y' shaped lower body. This is caused by spending so much time lying on their backs being serviced by all other *musica* and *submusica* species.

Sexually, all *vocalis* are voracious. It is essential for them to reach orgasm 7 times daily at least or else weight gain (leading to certain death) may become inevitable.

Weight gain for *vocalis* indicates that their life is coming to an end. Instinctively realising this they try to accelerate the process by bingeing at expensive restaurants but become violent when looked at or photographed. Thankfully, the decline and eventual death of *vocalis* is a speedy process.

HABITS

Most of the day is spent preening themselves in front of the mirror. Here they can practise their favourite pose or facial expression. Many weeks can be spent practising just one smile or raised eyebrow. The affordability of the camcorder has only served to exacerbate the problem with many *vocalis* filming themselves and watching the videos for hours at a time.

Both sexes have identical habits, which can sometimes make sexual identification difficult. *Vocalis* themselves, in their quest for constant sexual gratification, have long abandoned worrying about which sex their partner is, so long as multiple orgasm is possible.

Vocalis craves attention and will do anything to draw normal *Homo sapiens* into their circle of acquaintances. All *Homo sapiens* needs to do in return is assure *vocalis* that they look and sound gorgeous on a minute by minute basis in return *vocalis* will give almost any sexual or financial favour.

FOOD

Picky eaters - nibbling at seeds and green salads only once they're assured of zero calories. Weight gain as mentioned earlier is a very serious, if not fatal condition for this species. For many addiction to cocaine is inevitable - the limited calorific value of the substance being sufficient for these vain creatures.

BREEDING

Vocalis are attracted to almost anything that moves. The sex of their partner is not important as sex is sex. High profile *vocalis* will always try to have sex with other *vocalis* of either sex, in the belief that it will further raise their profile and make them even more famous. When two *vocalis* of the opposite sex do unite the result is sadly nearly always stillborn, the infant simply unable to cope with the embarrassment. Those that survive are given names that will cause their death from embarrassment shortly after joining their first school.

WHERE IT IS FOUND

Unlike most other reptiles *vocalis* actually slow down during the day - they need neon and flash photography to really come to life. For this reason they are only ever found in the centre of large cities of the developed world. Here they play a game of cat and mouse with another strange, and as yet un-categorised species - the paparazzi photographer. The relationship *vocalis* have with these sleazy creatures is utterly bizarre. They hate them absolutely but need them totally. If a photographer should stray too close then the *vocalis* will instinctively lash out with claws unsheathed often inflicting terrible wounds. If the photographer stays his distance he will know that his every movement is monitored closely. The instinct that *vocalis* have for the moment when the camera shutter is about to open is incredible. From distances of up to 300 metres a *vocalis* can sense a photograph about to be taken - even from behind - swivel round to be captured with the right profile and well rehearsed smile. A *vocalis* in his or her prime can do this with astonishing speed and accuracy, a feat that no other species can achieve.

Vocalis Grand Poserus - The Stadium Vocalist

Vocalis grand poserus is now a common site. *Grand poserus* is not necessarily destined to become a big star and sing in giant stadiums. Naturally this is the hope of the proud parents on realising that they've given birth to a grand poserus. In their element of the big stage, these creatures are quite magnificent. Striding along a 70 foot wide stage, long golden, highly permed hair, caught by the giant wind machines blast. They might have been born with a microphone stand in one hand the way they twirl it around them, occasionally putting the mike close to their mouths and bellowing something unintelligible like "Hello Wembley, you aaaaawl right - yeah". They rarely sing as a rule, their role is simply to strut up and down fondling their willy and leering at girlies in the audience.

A *grand poserus* that is sadly not successful, is on the other hand a rather pathetic creature. His instinct is to believe that he's on the big stage wherever he is - he cannot help this.

99p A PINT!!

To everyone else you have a complete jerk with long golden hair, a tight body suit made out of his girlfriends old tights, tastelessly capped off with a bit of fake fur draped over each arm. Even when he's performing at the Frog and Lettuce in Peckham, he'll still instinctively shout, "Hello Wembley, you aaaaawl right - yeah".

His instincts are so powerful that he'll stride backwards and forwards across the tiny stage fondling his willy and leering at his girlfriend (she's the only girl there).

Females of the species are always shot at birth - the parents unable to imagine what might happen if they should ever make it to a stage and instinctively fondle themselves while leering at 15,000 blokes.

The good news here is that there are unlikely to ever be any pure-bred *grand poserus*.

Vocalis Grand Prattus - The Common Vocalist

Vocalis grand prattus is so common that further classification is generally used to identify the various breeds.

The most interesting of these are *Vocalis completeprattus eyebrowsus*, *Vocalis grand gingerprattus* and *Vocalis patheticprattus*. The rate at which the species breeds and cross breeds means that there is a need to constantly monitor and, is necessary, re-classify the sub species.

Completeprattus eyebrowsus is a particularly nasty species. A result of inbreeding, *eyebrowsus* is usually part of a large family and while his or her siblings may be perfectly sane, *eyebrowsus* is a danger to society. Violent and abusive by nature these creatures should never be approached and never photographed or interviewed unless under strictly controlled conditions. This

The horror on a mother's face on realising that she's just given birth to Vocalis Grand prattus.

typically involves darting the individual with enough opiates to bring down an elephant and laying on a crate of whiskey to maintain the mild sedation.

The physical attributes revolve around huge eyebrows which probably grew in an effort to disguise the eyes, which in common with other insane species are deep and menacing. Where the eyebrows are less pronounced, dark glasses must be worn or the creature would be too terrifying for normal people to look at.

Gingerprattus is fairly rare - although the female is as common as the male. The overriding characteristic of the breed, apart from being ginger, is a complete lack of modesty and reality. This is made more apparent by their egos which are completely out of proportion to their ability. They do have great talent when it comes to creating pain in their listeners. The better *gingerprattus* do this by expressing their distress at being born ginger haired. The less talented achieve a similar result by being embarrassingly bad.

This ability to make their audience cringe and squirm with embarrassment only seems to encourage gingerprattus to attempt other activities in the misguided belief that other people might actually give a damn.

Patheticus is almost always the result of cross-breeding between a female *vocalis* and an over-sexed actor. It has been difficult to establish this link because of the fathers' refusal to admit that he would ever have anything to do with a *vocalis*.

The offspring, *vocalis patheticus* is, like all *vocalis* species, incredibly vain. However, this vanity is always tinged with a lack of satisfaction with the way they are and the way they look. As a result they practise their pained expression for hours. The male is more common than the female. This probably explains why they cross-dress - frilly shirts (no doubt for easy lifting) and leather trousers are *de rigeur*. They'll spend hours making up and having their hair done. Female *patheticus* is just as sad in her way and is characterised by the ability to write and perform excruciatingly bad lyrics. Only *gingerprattus* can make the audience cringe more than female *patheticus*.

Vocalis Grand Bitchus - The Diva

Vocalis grand bitchus are probably the most dangerous of all vocalis. They can kill in many ways - a bad performance, with their tongue, their eyes and with their extremely sharp claws. As with *Vocalis complete prattus eyebrowsus*, *grand bitchus* is best approached only when heavily sedated. Over 98% of the species is female, the male only occasionally survives as he'll typically be savagely killed by his sister while still in his cot.

Vocalis grand bitchus need to start young to have any chance of survival in the wild. Often thrust on stage while still only 6 or 7 years old these *grand bitchus* brats screech at an annoyingly loud volume in talent competitions across the developed world. It's backstage in small competitions that they can practise their quick turn and look that can turn

homo sapiens to stone if they dare criticise the performance. They also develop their lethal put down lines at an early age. Fortunately, their claws do not develop until puberty so their bark is worse than their bite when young.

Puberty is the signal to start trawling around the record companies. Here they must learn to be nice to people - or at least pretend. For most this simply goes against the grain and, however badly they want to be successful just can't stop bitching.

Record company executives will always (from behind a protective screen) reject *grand bitchus* first time as a ploy to see if they can act nicely when they want to. This will be essential for those endless interviews when they must look like nice to other people in front of camera.

Although a failed *grand bitchus* is a terrifying site when met down a dark alley, she is nothing compared to successful *grand bitchus* - a normal person would survive a matter of minutes only. They must be constantly supervised by their record company who, fearing huge law suits from s e r i o u s l y injured fans, must provide a huge entourage to protect the public from ever coming into contact directly with *grand bitchus*.

The entourage must be constantly m a i n t a i n e d because of killing and serious injury within the camp. A mature *grand bitchus* is capable of destroying an entire entourage in an afternoon of savagery. A dresser or

hairdresser is likely to be the spark for a tantrum - and of course the first casualty. Usually verbal abuse is sufficient to put down a hairdresser. If the hairdresser survives this and tries to make a run for it then he or she will certainly be cut down by the claws.

Once *grand bitchus* has tasted blood she may be difficult to s t o p.

Accountants and road managers have little chance against a raging *grand bitchus*. The only hope for an entourage is to hide in cupboards in the hope that *grand bitchus* will gradually tire of the slaughter and drown her sorrows with several bottles of vodka and a tub of Valium.

Vocalis noconceptofpitchus - The Can't Sing On Their Own Vocalist

Noconceptofpitchus have many variants. Males and females abound in roughly equal numbers. When isolated these sad creatures will simply run around in circles with their arms outstretched playing aeroplanes and making silly noises. They are perfectly harmless when kept isolated from others of their kind.

The problem for the rest of us is when they get together. Two are usually fairly subdued but when three or more get together they may start singing. In the misguided belief that they are singing in tune and actually harmonising with each other they may start to record a demo tape and try and get a record deal. In the wild they would be so bad that they'd never succeed. However, in recent times unscrupulous *Homo submusica hangersonus insidius* and *fleecus* (page 76) have intentionally brought these normally isolated creatures together. The result has been a disaster for good tasteful music, seemingly thousands of boy and girl bands made up of *noconceptofpitchus*. Sometimes attempts were made to mix male and female *noconceptofpitchus* together with obvious consequences. Even without being

A group of noconceptofpitchus on a photo shoot

intentionally brought together the sheer number of these groups has meant that many *noconceptofpitchus* marriages have taken place. We simply do not know what kind of offspring will be produced. The idea that male and female *noconceptofpitchus* should mate has been taboo for centuries. The reason for this taboo is not really understood but it is thought that some kind of creature resembling a cross between *grand bitchus* and *noconceptofpitchus* would be the result.

We are now entering a very dangerous era for tasteful music. *Noconceptofpitchus* groups have been so well marketed and exploited by species of *Hangersonus*, that it has been possible for individual members of these hideous groups to make a go of a solo career.

This has not been easy for the various *Hangersonus* to bring about. Sure, it's fairly easy to fake, I mean make a record, using an individual *noconceptofpitchus* but how do they get away with it live. This requires a major cheat. It's never hard for *Hangersonus* to bribe *musica* species to play in a show, so there's no problem putting a band together. To achieve a vocal effect however, banks of backing *vocalis* are required. This is not easy to arrange. Most self-respecting *vocalis* (if that's not a contradiction in terms) will refuse point blank to do the job. After all they want to be a star themselves, why should they be used to promote some prat or bimbo *noconceptofpitchus*. As with most things in life, money eventually solves the problem. However, usually the only bribable females are failed *grand bitchus* and usually only *clubarsolorus* will be bribed on the male side.

The problems of handling a large group of backing vocalis consisting of these two breeds makes you wonder whether it's all worth the effort.

Vocalis pututosleepus - Jazz Club Vocalists

Vocalis pututosleepus are really any type of vocalis that have the power to anaesthetise normal people.

They are physically very frail and must spend much of the day in a large box filled with cotton wool in case they should fall asleep without realising it and possibly hurt themselves. There has always been a ready market for this species. A must for those smoky jazz clubs and dives the species is also frequently successful as a recording artist. Hugely laid back records that soothe people into slumber.

With the big stars live appearances are rare because of the difficulty in arranging sleeping facilities for several thousand people.

Pututosleepus need to develop strong solo skills as the power of their singing will frequently put the band to sleep as well as the audience.

Vocalis bimbosexus - The Bimbo Vocalist

Vocalis bimbosexus is probably one of the most ancient species of *Vocalis*. Since the dawn of time *Homo sapiens* would much rather watch some gorgeous bit of crumpet perform than a truly fine singer - who cares what it sounds like so long as she goes like a train.

Over the centuries the breed has been perfected to produce a thin reedy voice, huge tits - with matching eyes, full rounded lips and an arse to die for. Amazingly there are many males of the species - originally allowed to live to help keep the breed pure - many have themselves made it in showbiz. Often they become foppish game show hosts or cabaret singers. Instead of huge tits they have huge bums. The breed is in some danger due to the unwillingness of the females to mate with their pure bred but foppish males.

Like all *vocalis*, *bimbosexus* is incredibly vain but stupid with it. They'll buy dogs that match their hair. They'll have their limos resprayed to match whatever outfit they've just bought.

Bimbosexus is perfectly harmless, they have some fairly savage put down lines that they use when cornered but have no appetite for violence in the way that *grand bitchus* has. This makes them very popular with chat show hosts who can flirt and make innuendo for hours, *bimbosexus* will remain cute at all times.

Vocalis grand prattus poseursuperiore - **Painfully Posing Vocalists**

Vocalis grand prattus poseursuperiore is probably the ultimate *vocalis*. They have every typical *vocalis* attribute in overload. Vanity is unbridled; successful *grand prattus poseursuperiore* will have a huge entourage which are required 24 hours a day. Included in the entourage will be P.A., assistant to P.A., consultant hairstylist, several assistant hairstylists, wind machine operator, make up consultant and assistants, dietitian, personal trainer, accountants, financial advisors, managers, road managers and many more too numerous to mention. The males of the species are especially over the top and will expect a hareem to be provided at every gig. Their diet of cocaine and vodka is supplemented only by the occasional carrot.

The only redeeming feature is that usually they can actually sing. Remember that vocal ability is not what classifies a *vocalis*. The males in particular would never be tolerated without vocal prowess.

Vocalis clubarsolorus - The Club Vocalist

Clubarsolorus is at the opposite end of the scale from *grand prattus poseursuperiore*. The really sad thing about them is that they possess what should be everything *vocalis*, except that nothing works in practice except the true *vocalis* cheesy smile. Whenever they try to sing, out comes an impression of the intended song that only a cat or a dog might recognise. Many venues exploit this by having 'guess the song' competitions.

Like all *vocalis* their vanity exceeds everything else in their life. They truly believe that they can sing, entertain and be casually amusing. Of course, they believe right up to their death bed that they have film star looks. This refusal to accept reality, even through old age, explains why so many wrinkly bastards are still performing in dingy clubs up and down the land.

The number of *clubarsolorus* is now becoming a worry for most western governments who are faced with the dilemma over whether or not to organise a mass cull. Clearly this would be a popular policy. However, *clubarsolorus* may suffer from serious delusions of grandeur but they're not stupid. It is believed that they have formed a secret society that has infiltrated every area of the establishment - including government. Little wonder that what for many is a simple solution to the crisis of overpopulation of this sad species, is being delayed.

ORIGIN

Gitus have evolved slowly, probably originating from northern and central Europe. At first they were nomadic peoples moving humbly from public house to public house playing to earn just enough money to get pissed. In this respect little has changed over hundreds of years. The modern guitarist began to evolve when a small group of crap, outlawed guitarists stowed away on a ship bound for the new world to escape an angry mob they'd cheated getting a dance gig. On a cold January morning in 1721 these brave pioneers arrived in what is now known as New York. Apart from a record of their arrival little is known about them after that,

other than they must have put it about a bit, as soon after there were guitarists springing up around camp fires all across the new world.

However, the general temperament of the guitarist was still broadly the same, humble folk strumming a few chords for a beer and beans. Slowly, the blues influenced the way guitarists played, enabling them to occasionally express emotion. By the middle of the nineteenth century almost every family had a guitar player in its midst. *Gitus* has spread so rapidly because of their attraction to *Homo sapiens*. They have a strong desire to mate with any *sapiens* they can, although they will pure breed too. However, cross-breeding is a constant threat to mainstream *Homo sapiens* society today with no solution to the problem.

Today, as we know only too well, *Gitus* are dominated by electric guitarists. The origins of this disturbed species lay in the early 20th century when some well intentioned guitar maker decided to add pick-ups to the guitar and connect the whole thing to an amplifier. Originally conceived as a way of lifting the humble and gentle acoustic guitar within the jazz combo so that it was audible. However, like so many inventions of the 20th century the creator of the electric guitar could not have foreseen that his discovery would end up being used as a weapon of mass destruction - destroying ear drums and the lives of young people all across the globe.

SIZE and GENERAL ANATOMY

As the electric guitar evolved so did a completely new breed of guitarist. Accelerated by cross-breeding with vocalists this new breed of guitarist grew up without a frontal lobe and rapidly evolved thick skin tissue within the ear canal enabling them to cope with volumes fatal to all other species. The male is generally brightly coloured and loud, the female rarely asserts herself and is merely a drab copy of the male.

There are many breeds of *Gitus* too numerous to mention but they are bound by a common thread. A burning desire to show-off and be loud

HABITAT

Easily the most widely dispersed of all *Homo musica*. Such has been their success in cross-breeding with *Homo sapiens* that perhaps as many as 80% of adults in the developed world have cross-bred with a *Gitus*.

HABITS

No longer shy, humble creatures happy to play for a pint of beer and a bed for the night, they spend most of the day sleeping, waking only when others return from work to rest. This is the wake up call to most guitarists to get up, switch on their amplifier to full volume and then 'practise' until midnight or later.

Their 'practise' sessions are incredibly repetitive and annoying for anyone in earshot. Hours of string bending into long held notes that eventually blister into hideous feedback squeals. These squealing noises have become more elaborate as guitarists evolve ridiculous techniques and have been made really annoying with the invention of the floating tremolo arm.

Gitus are obsessed with any machine that can further distort and alter their sound thereby enhancing the pain for everyone else. Echo effects that nature never intended are now common place - the ability to sample short phrases of lead solos so that they can be endlessly repeated, has driven many weaker species to commit suicide at an alarming rate. Many of the smaller species of *Vocalis* have been wiped out in as little as 25 years and *Blowjobus saxus* numbers may never recover.

FOOD

Almost any food is taken, swallowed whole and washed down with neat whiskey or bourbon. Cannabis and amphetamines are essential supplements with cocaine optional for successful players.

BREEDING

The male of the species outnumbers the female by about 5:1. Rarely is the male attracted to the female of the species preferring to further cross-breed with *Homo sapiens*.

WHERE IT IS FOUND

Gitus is so widely dispersed around the globe that you are just as likely to have your eardrums assaulted in a quiet country pub as in the centre of a large city.

Gitus volumus obsessivus - The Rock Guitarist

Gitus volumus obsessivus is one of the most dangerous of the *Gitus* family. A cross-breed between female *Gitus pubus* and *Vocalis grand prattus* which produces *Gitus* as young as 6 years old. By the time they're 13 or 14 they've already developed the distinctive thick padded ear canals and sloped foreheads so typical of this breed. With the protective padding fully developed they can reach screechingly loud volumes on a daily basis.

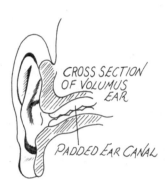

CROSS SECTION OF VOLUMUS EAR.

PADDED EAR CANAL

On a more positive note this breed does usually learn to play quite impressively and their life, indeed their whole religion is based around worshipping the guitar and former guitar gods. Their worship ritual is passed down from mother to child and usually revolves around a gigantic, slightly frayed poster of Hendrix. Mother and child will then sit around a table positioned so they can see the poster with incense burning and Voodoo Chile playing at maximum volume.

You may be wondering what role the father plays in the development of young *Gitus volumus obsessivus*. The

The young Gitus voluminus obsessivus at prayer.

answer is none. *Vocalis grand prattus* will almost certainly leave his partner upon hearing she's five months pregnant and so plays no part in the upbringing. In some cases the distraught female *Gitus pubus* may seek the male of her species to help rear the little bastard. This is rarely very successful as he's usually too busy down the pub to be bothered.

By the time *volumus obsessivus* is about 16 or 17 years old - provided he's had a strict religious upbringing - he (or she) is likely to be a very impressive player. He will rise through the ranks of bands possibly joining a band on the verge of signing a record deal while still in his teens. His mother, *Gitus pubus*, never achieved this status (see *Gitus pubus*) and so is totally supportive, happy to become an expensive prostitute to fund the blossoming career of her loud offspring.

By the time our hero is nearing his mid-twenties he's close to burn out. Sadly, *volumus obsessivus* is destined to die young (yes, there really is a God, thank you). Most of the species that b e c o m e successful will be completely unable to handle the fame becoming wrapped up in the rock ethic of sex, drugs and rock and roll. They simply want more and more and although they often become genuinely brilliant guitarists and musicians, they also become more and more alcohol and drug dependent. They need almost as much sex as *Vocalis grand prattus* and simply cannot quit or cut back.

Mercifully, the end when it comes is quick. Drunk with success, the now ridiculously o v e r c o n f i d e n t *volumus obsessivus* simply goes too far one day. Many believe that Hendrix will save them if they step off a 12 storey balcony or that it will make a great end of show effect to wire their guitar direct to the mains - how the audience went wild as *voluminus* fried.

Gitus Volumus obsessivus - R.I.P.

Gitus Pubus - The Semi-pro Pub Guitarist

Gitus pubus is without doubt the most annoying - albeit harmless member of the *Gitus* family. Many are 40 or 50 years old and still atrociously bad at playing guitar.

Their big problem is that they just can't accept how bad they are. They virtually force their way into bands of young musicians easily impressed with their experience on the road. This probably amounts to 20 gigs in as many years but in that time they may have failed to learn how to play guitar but have mastered bullshit.

Even when young the males go bald. In typical fashion they cannot accept this and spend the rest of their lives keeping the rest of their hair as long as possible, some even combing a few strands across their bald patch. Their dress sense at gigs is appalling. Tight spandex trousers usually with a tiger stripe or glitter effect. They wear these for the remainder of their gigging life. In some extreme cases the trousers are never washed, *pubus* believing that this might be bad luck.

They fail totally with the opposite sex until well into their thirties. They only begin to attract females then because they are the only species prepared to listen to the abuse stories of female *Gitus pubus* now that she's been left by *Vocalis grand prattus*.

This ability to listen or pretend to listen to female *Gitus* of all species has more or less guaranteed the success of the breed. Worse still for the rest of us it means the breed will remain pure.

Their one redeeming feature is their ability to be either unaware or to totally ignore abuse and insults from the audience. This means they're very entertaining and can be heckled with no fear of reprisal.

Gitus dormusbullshitus - The Bedroom (thinks he's a genius) Guitarist

Without doubt the saddest of all the *Gitus* family is *dormusbullshitus*. Yes they're dedicated to guitar but as they never quite achieve the standard of their heroes, they will never venture out into the world. Join a band - forget it - their inadequacies would be immediately apparent. So they get good enough that anyone passing by their window will know they play guitar. This gives them just enough confidence to get down the pub (guitar safely locked in bedroom) and spend the entire night telling everyone how good they are and slagging off all the greats.

Their favourite line is how they'd mastered everything

Clapton's ever recorded by the time they were 12. Even more annoyingly they almost always have a dream guitar collection and drone on for hours about why a 62 strat isn't a patch an a '59. Oh and their '59 just happened to belong to Elvis and it's still got some lyposuction residue stuck to the bridge saddles, blah blah blah all evening!

Gitus dormabullshitus practising.

Gitus bluus suicidus - **The Blues Guitarist**

This ancient, slowly evolving species is generally well liked by both *sapiens* and *musica*. Gentle and harmless, these creatures are exploited by everyone; women, vocalists, record company executives, publishers and landlords. You name them, *bluus suicidus* has been abused by them.

Born direct into the ghetto, life starts badly and then rapidly goes downhill. There are very few females of the species so pure bred specimens are hard to find. The male only carries the *bluus* gene and so his partner can come from almost any human or *musica* source.

Females are sometimes born and reared but rarely making a mark as a blues guitarist as they are usually driven into prostitution by unscrupulous agents.

Males usually drift from one city to another seeking their fortune but only finding despair. They crave stability but their self-destructive nature means that even when they find the perfect woman they simply have to be unfaithful until she walks out, leaving the male distraught and racked with guilt. They desire good health but cannot resist poisoning themselves with cheap liquor. They live in cheap rented r o o m s knowing that they'll be evicted any day. If they're not evicted then there's something wrong with the building and, fearing for their lives, *bluus suicidus* runs to the next city and the next gig.

Of course all this suffering is essential if *bluus suicidus* is to become a really fine blues guitarist. But they are seldom discovered and become big stars. Even when a genuine *bluus* is discovered there is no happiness or rest for them. They continue to be ripped off by society, their new manager, their new record company, their new ex-model girlfriend - even their own dog continues to pee on their bed.

They achieve fulfilment in life by playing guitar. Success is irrelevant here because all blues players close their eyes and go into a trance as soon as they bend a string. Suddenly all their years of suffering is worthwhile, the audience being carried along on an emotional rollercoaster. Naturally it helps, if at the end, there is a deafening roar of a huge crowd rather than

the sound of someone vomiting in a corner as the barman claps apologetically.

Bluus suicidus is probably only surpassed emotionally by *Blowjobus saxus selfdestructus* and *Screechus violinii wailingwallus.*

They have many imitators. Many lesser breeds of *gitus* can copy much of what *bluus suicidus* does and although they can never reproduce exactly the true *bluus* emotion, their superior skills in dealing with life and business mean they often get more attention than *bluus suicidus*. This is a further blow to *bluus*, now they're even ripped off mercilessly by their own kind. Certainly everyone else seems to get paid more and more often than not they get laid more as well.

At the present time *bluus* numbers are substantial and the breed is not in any danger, however, it is my opinion that unless the breed is helped to remain pure and imitators controlled (preferably culled), the breed will soon become endangered.

Gitus woolycardius & ooharntaecleverus - The Jazz Guitarist

Ooharntaecleverus is the sort of smarmy smart-arse you really wish you'd never got into conversation with. Very similar in manner to many *Ivorytinklus* they know absolutely everything about music and about the guitar. They also believe they know everything about everyone else's instrument. They know every song and can play every song in any key.

Their comping (accompaniment to you and me) is oh so clever, with chord voicings that they've never played before but just came to them at that moment. Worse still is their insistence on showing everyone their new chord shape and instructing everyone else how to react to it.

As you might imagine many are sent into exile

where no one understands a word they say. In extreme cases they are often brutally murdered for being so bloody clever. If *ooharntaecleverus* has been so wrapped up in his or her own genius that they've failed to notice that the drummer is perhaps a *technosoprettius* or even *commonasmuckus* then they could be in real danger.

Woolycardius, on the other hand, is totally harmless and very unassuming, quietly getting on with his gentle solos and cheesy, mellow chord changes. Although probably as clever as his relative, *ooharntaecleverus*, *woolycardius* never really brags or lets on that he's actually rather good. This does mean that they're destined, like many jazz players, to remain obscure.

Gitus anaesthetisus - The Meaningless Guitarist

Closely related to some species of *Saxus*, *Gitus anaesthetisus* has emerged, probably a cross breed between either *ooharntae-cleverus* and *Vocalis pututosleepus*. The resulting offspring have very worrying characteristics. They have the quiet vanity of *pututosleepus* with the smarmy arrogance of *ooharntaecleverus*. Worse still they lack *ooharntae-cleverus'* imagination and musical skill, using what talent they have to try and put everyone in earshot into a trance of utter boredom.

This musical equivalent of a lobotomy is made worse by the appalling dress sense and old fashioned hair styles. They try to make a performance when playing live but only end up looking utter prats. This does give the audience something to laugh about but the blandness of the music wins through in the end with thousands of innocent people bored to death.

Gitus aahnbeeus poserus - The Big Show Guitarist

The result of a nuclear accident in the mid 1960's, *aahnbeeus poserus* suddenly emerged in huge numbers. A large herd of *Bluus suicidus* appears to have been showered with radiation and full of confidence bred like rabbits with many different species of *Vocalis* females.

Big hair, big dicks (so they say) and a big guitar sound are their trademarks. Sometimes confused with *Gitus voluminus obsessivus* the breed can usually be told apart by the strong blues influence in their playing.

Everything they do is a performance. Don't go to the gents toilet with males of the species as he'll turn it into a 10 minute spectacular featuring the long distance urinating competition.

They wear anything that glitters. They decorate their guitars with sequins and shells and old, highly polished bullet casings.

Gitus pretenditsartyarsolorus - The Indie Punk Guitarist

God only knows where this breed has come from, thicker than most species of *Drummus*, they rely utterly on heavy distortion and volume.

They imagine that they're super-cool and utterly rebellious. The fact is that they're still living with their mum when they turn 35.

Their background of art college, they believe, gives them the right to play any crap and call it art. Most bands need about three of them to create a coherent sound as none of them can play with any consistency, so they need several to cover all the gaps and mistakes.

Gitus borustodeathus - The Folk Guitarist

Occasionally throughout history, some *Gitus* have become isolated and have regressed, herding sheep or cattle and playing for their own pleasure at the evening meal.

Their descendants, uncomfortable with modern life, play only acoustic instruments and always sing (dreadfully) along while they play. Total drivel to the rest of us - either sung in an accent, or with lyrics that no one else can ever understand.

ORIGIN

Drummus are thought to originate from the African sub-continent in about 2 BC. Around 50 BC hordes of swarthy drummers beat a path to northern Europe beating, hitting and tapping on every table in their path. It was only when they reached northern Europe in about 112 AD that the damp and cold slowed them down sufficiently for other rapidly evolving musicians to persuade and eventually train them to hit only tuned percussion instruments.

The word drummer comes from the Latin; *Drummus* - literally 'to beat the living crap out of'. The general species *Drummus* has many variations from the truly dreadful *Drummus noconceptoftimus* to the colourful, almost musical *Drummus technosoprettius*.

SIZE and GENERAL ANATOMY

Generally larger than *Homo musica* most species are physically well developed with legs like kangaroos and the arms of a chimpanzee on steroids. The brain of course is almost nonexistent [fig 1.], Providing enough impulses to hit things and open their mouths to take in the vast quantity of lager needed to sustain them through a rehearsal or gig. When you compare their brain size to that of an *Ivorytinklus*, for example you wonder whether they have the brains to take a pee without assistance. In fact, *drummus* is remarkably intelligent when compared to frogs and birds and other animals with a similar brain size. With a good upbringing, most *drummus* can learn to dress themselves and communicate in a basic way, such as "ella", which most experienced off-licence managers know means, 'please may I have a large case of Stella'.

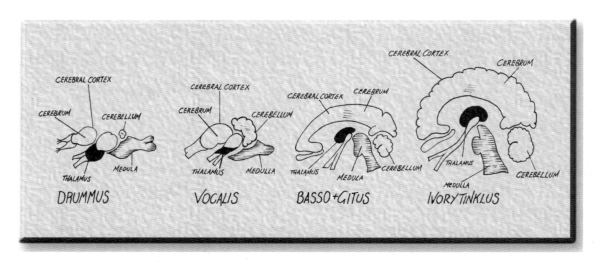

fig.1

Although *Drummus* have small eyes set well back into the skull they probably only see in black and

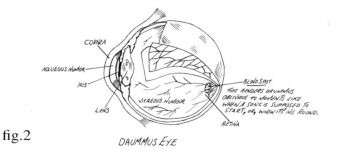

fig.2

CORNEA

AQUEOUS HUMOR

IRIS

LENS

VITREOUS HUMOUR

BLIND SPOT
THIS RENDERS DRUMMUS
OBLIVIOUS TO MOMENTS LIKE
WHEN A SONG IS SUPPOSED TO
START, OR, WHEN ITS HIS ROUND.

RETINA

DRUMMUS EYE

white, which probably explains their completely vacant expression when other musicians are discussing tone colour. Their hearing, although keen when it's someone else's round, is generally poor and really only picks up basic vibrations hence their need to hit the drums so damn hard.

FOOD

Most species of *Drummus* can survive on a diet of approximately 90% lager, as long as its export strength, 5% amphetamines and 5% vindaloo. Many breeds of *drummus* will indulge in recreational drugs and always smoke hundreds of roll-ups a day. However, most drugs have little or no additional effect when taken in conjunction with the large quantities of lager required daily by all breeds of *drummus*. This is because there is only so much abuse a small *drummus* brain can take before it simply shuts down into unconsciousness.

BREEDING

Fortunately breeding *Drummus* are rare as they are usually too pissed to get around to it. Also the female of the species is quite rare and usually lesbian so that pure bred *Drummus* are almost unheard of. Most breeds of *drummus* also lack any sort of social skills that enable many *musica* and *submusica* species to cross-breed with *Homo sapiens* for example. Leering and vomiting over female *sapiens* rarely gets *drummus* a bedroom invite. This particular approach is though typical only of *D. commonasmuckus* and *D. noconceptoftimus*. Breeds like *D. technosoprettius* and, in their own way *D. technosmartarsus* can learn to copy many social skills - sufficient to pull anyway.

WHERE IT IS FOUND

Widely distributed around much of the developed world *Drummus* can be found almost anywhere, usually under tables and park benches when not gigging or rehearsing. They can be found in rural areas as well as in towns and cities and generally adapt well to a variety of habitats, unlike much of *Homo musica* and *submusica*. They only require deaf neighbours, an off-licence and an Indian take-away to survive - although only the off-licence is an absolute requirement all year round.

Drummus gadgetasaurus - The Equipment Fetish Drummer

Gadgetasaurus is an easy species to identify even for the novice. There are records of *gadgetasaurus* from Roman times. Although not as easy to spot in these times, *gadgetasaurus* could be seen bolting his drum to his shield to enable him to protect himself while drumming. Those *drummus* who needed to hold their drums with one hand and beat with the other found the drum rather poor at stopping arrows from penetrating their heart. The success of the species was more or less guaranteed by its success in the battlefield.

The modern gadgetasaurus is very easy to spot, thanks to modern technology. Today drummers have specially made gloves (presumably this is to ensure they don't drop their sticks, as it's much less painful removing sticks that have been stuck to gloves with superglue than those that have been stuck direct to the fleshy palms of hands). So, clearly *gadgetasaurus* is a thinking drummer, albeit in a limited way.

Gadgetasaurus have drinks holders that can be clamped to their hi-hat stands (cans only), (those drummers that need intravenous lager drips still need a converted cymbal stand).

Despite being naturally stupid, *gadgetasaurus* is incredibly imaginative when it comes to making life easier. They have foot pedals that not only allow them to control high hat, five kick drums and a lavatory flush, from one single pedal, but also they can flick a switch and a new set of drum sticks is fired towards them with great accuracy. Sadly *gadgetasaurus* may forget this and end up speared by the graphite tipped sticks, rather than catch them.

Their invention of different types of stand is truly incredible. Some have stands that hold two tomtoms, a crash cymbal, a drinks cabinet, a music stand and an oxyacetylene welding kit.

Gadgetasaurus is inevitably going to have the biggest kit, with the most accessories. Two, sometimes three kick drums, at least 8 tomtoms, preferably 12. A triple rotating hi-hat (three different types of hi-hat cymbals on a single rotating stand. Gloves, drumming trousers, tank top with Paiste emblazoned across it, six lager can holders placed equally around the kit. Drumming helmet (a throw back from Roman times) now used to prevent injury from the automatic drumstick launcher. A multi function floor pedal, a drum stool commode so that body functions can be performed at any time. Cans (headphones) so that they can pretend they give a damn about what the rest of the band are up to. Attached to this is a small microphone so that they can bellow obscenities whilst pretending to do backing vocals. They must have at least 6 cymbals although in extreme cases this figure may easily double. Even though they don't really play percussion, *gadgetasaurus* must have all sorts of percussion instruments. Rarely are these played and even more rarely understood but boy does percussion add to the equipment list of *gadgetasaurus*.

They also attach certain percussion instruments to their kit, using their welding equipment. These items include cow bells, triangles and car hub caps.

Drummus technoshitus - The Overcomplicated Drummer

Technoshitus has a larger brain than is usually found in the greater *drummus* species. However, rather than use this brain power to do something sensible, like get a job, *technoshitus* spends at least 17 hours a day practising.

Unfortunately for the rest of society, they don't practise anything that we want to hear, like great time-keeping or great feel. No, *technoshitus* practises outrageous and completely unusable fills and patterns. They can play nine notes per bar with their right hand on the toms, against a sixteenth note pattern with their left hand while playing a waltz with their feet. Why, who knows. Why are these bastards allowed to live after birth - they should be put down.

Physically, *technoshitus* is obsessed with himself (nearly all *technoshitus* are male). They spend much of their spare time in the gym, although unlike *drummus technosoprettius*, only non-drumming spare time. For *technoshitus*, physical development is simply to aid their drum skills as they never look in the mirror or try to pick up women. Try to understand, this species only drum, nothing else.

Drummus technosmartarsus - The Oh So Clever Jazzy Drummer

Technosmartarsus has probably the largest brain of all *Drummus*. And boy, does he (or she, as females are not uncommon) let you know they have some brain cells. Their eyes are set back further than in most *drummus* and their eyesight is usually poor. In modern times this is no problem as they simply bolt on h u g e l y p o w e r f u l glasses. They can, when it suits them, fake total blindness. This they do to appear even more sincere than they'd otherwise be.

They differ from most other species of *drummus* by being almost musical. They are not classified *musica*, still *submusica drummus* but are regarded as considerably more musical than *Gitus pubus*, for example.

They are easy to spot as they hold their sticks funny (sorry, properly). The novice may confuse them with some *drummus commonasmuckus* who try to appear cleverer than they really are by copying *technosmartarsus*.

Techno-smartarsus' favourite trick is to try and catch *basso complex* napping (*Basso simplex* would not be tolerated) by playing some ridiculous rhythm pattern before returning to normal two bars later. If the *basso* is still with them then they're given the cheesy smile of approval, which *technosmartarsus* thinks will make it all worthwhile. The smarmier the *technosmartarsus*, the more likely this trick will be repeated.

Drummus technosoprettius - **The Vain Drummer**

Technosoprettius is closely related to *technosmartarsus*. Possibly, there is *vocalis* blood from previous generations. Their obsession with everything drums is only exceeded by their obsession with themselves. They possibly have the genes to be as technically proficient as *technosmartarsus* but spend too much time in the gym or at the hairdressers to develop their talent for drumming fully.

To innocent *s a p i e n s ,* *technosoprettius* will always win readers polls for best drummer. They are tricked, of course, mirrors and complex video screens ensure that the audience can see every aspect of *technosoprettius'* playing.

Technosoprettius is a master poser. He can peer coyishly between the curls of his perm at camera 1, whilst simultaneously doing paradiddles across his huge tomtom collection. He can hold his sticks up just that little bit too long if it means that his biceps will be lit up perfectly.

Unlike *Vocalis*, *technosoprettius* doesn't have any natural instinct for a photographer, so instead must pose at full stretch all the time. Every crash cymbal is hit unnecessarily hard, the features creasing up just enough to look hard, but not so much that the camera won't catch the glint in his eye.

The female of the species approaches her prettiness differently. They simply wear low cut tee-shirts that exaggerate their cleavage. Every move is made to support this, admittedly fine feature of their performance.

Drummus noconceptoftimus - The Crap Drummer

Drummus noconceptoftimus is a sad, pathetic creature. All the *drummus* species have, as we've discussed earlier, smaller brains than most other species. *Noconceptoftimus* not only has a the

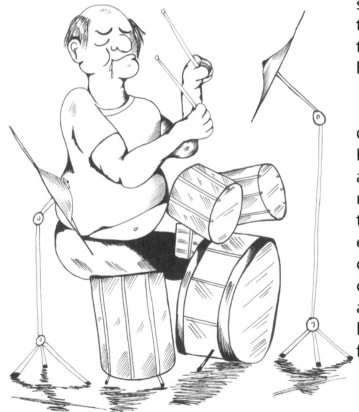

You may be wondering why they're tolerated at all by other *musica* and *submusica* species. The answer is that they are not tolerated by any *musica* with any talent. The problem is, that a great many species of *musica* have the same absence of time keeping skills as *noconceptoftimus* and therefore tolerate him or her in the forlorn hope that they'll get better with practise.

This is unlikely, as *noconceptoftimus* doesn't understand what it is to practise. He lives for the rehearsal and (God help us all) the gig. Mention the idea of using a metronome or drum machine to improve their time-keeping would be greeted by an epileptic-type fit of drum fills - hopelessly out of time, followed by the instinctive comment "I wouldn't want to ruin my feel and become a machine". The only solution here is to machine gun the bastard to death for the sake of all human kind.

smallest brain of any of the *drummus* species but has no cerebral cortex - well, none worth mentioning anyway.

Drummus commonasmuckus - **The Common Pub Drummer**

Drummus commonasmuckus is closely related to *Drummus noconceptoftimus*. The big difference is that *commonasmuckus* has a normal *drummus* brain and so can improve a little by practise and hard work. Not all of them choose to do this and you can then only tell them apart from their truly pathetic cousins in conversation, which will be lively and filled with jokes (albeit old ones), told at length and with gusto.

Their appetite for life is immense. Where as most *drummus* can get through an evening of gigging or rehearsing with a single case of Stella, *commonasmuckus* will arrive with one or two kegs to see him through the night. Such is the need for excessive alcohol that it is very common - even in a gig - for the drumming to be cut back to feet and one hand - normal drum pattern minus the hi-hat. The right hand is well developed for

drinking. Obviously this is a really revolting sight for anyone else as half the tankard is slopped over *commonasmuckus* and the floor. With the more imaginative *commonasmuckus*, the audience will hardly notice, this is because most of the drum parts have little or no hi-hat patterns in them at all, enabling the free hand to pour, uncork, and drink without interrupting the band.

So common is this breed that, in common with breeds, such as *Basso simplex steadyasarockus*, large groups of out of work *commonasmuckus* will gather whenever one of them has a gig. They'll cheer any mistake and constantly suggest alternative parts and fills by doing their own table top drumming.

Normally *commonasmuckus* is placid but when in large groups drinking constantly, this can change rapidly. All it takes is a bit of an error from the playing *commonasmuckus* and the others will almost bring the roof down with a drunken roar of hysterical laughter. The playing *commonasmuckus* is unable to take this level of insult and hurls himself off the stage bodily into the general area of the watching *commonasmuckus* table. Within

seconds there is absolute carnage. Blood, bone, lager and broken wood and glass everywhere.

Sadly for the playing *commonasmuckus* he's a bit outnumbered and so is beaten to a pulp, regretting his pride the following morning. Fortunately *drummus* of all breeds are genetically adapted for fighting. Their small brains and little used genitals mean that serious injury is rare, they usually don't even realise they've been in a fight the following morning, all they experience is a slightly worse hangover than usual.

Of course the throng of watching *commonasmuckus* have good reason to beat the playing *drummus* to a pulp. They want to get up and play themselves. At some point during the fight one of the *commonasmuckus* will steal himself away from the fight and sneak up to the drum kit. The band begin playing again - none the worse for a change of *commonasmuckus*.

It is not uncommon for this scene to be repeated three or four times in one gig. Such is the short tempered nature of the drunken *commonasmuckus*.

ORIGIN

Basso originally came from central Africa. *Basso* can be traced back to about 50 BC. The pure bred *basso* always lived on the fringes of large forests where they could roam the grasslands by day and, as evening fell, could move close to the forest where they could use their height to feed from the trees at the forest's edge. In about 2 BC it is thought a group of *basso* were captured and used by the Romans in their quest to expand their empire across the globe. A Roman legion simply needed one bassist and one drummer. On surrounding a town or city they wanted to capture they simply made it clear that as soon as the drum solo stopped it was time for the bass solo. At which point the entire population would stream out of the town knowing that certain death at the hands of the Romans would be a far quicker and more noble death than listening to a bass solo that could, if the *basso* was good, last for hours.

In around 10 BC it is known that a group of pure bred *basso* were either captured or isolated from their main group. Either because they were forced or became desperate in isolation, this group cross-bred with chimpanzees. The result is what we now call *Basso simplex*.

SIZE and GENERAL ANATOMY

The pure bred male *Basso* is at least 7 feet tall usually with a hair style that increases their height by at least another foot. The female is almost as tall but they tend to have wide hair in order to distinguish themselves from the male. Although generally slim, *Basso* can sometimes become over shy and hide themselves away almost always leading to obesity. They usually become phenomenal bass players in this state but are so shy that they'll rarely venture onto the concert stage.

HABITAT

Now widely dispersed across much of the globe *basso* especially the pure bred specimens still need their grazing area. Often they will frequent parks and other open spaces, milling around usually on their own or occasionally in small groups, the male will spend months walking the same route in the forlorn hope that one day a female will ask him to join her band.

HABITS

Joining a band is always the main aim of *basso*. The male and female of the species all seek this goal. They must do all they can to be noticed by other musicians - as long as it doesn't involve travelling too far. They will spend hours creating great looking adverts to put up in shop windows. Their hope is that when a band realises that it is just going to have to get a bassist they will simply call the ad that looks best and ask the bassist to join over the phone.

FOOD

Because of their diet of grass, *basso* must eat continuously to keep up their body weight and have just enough energy to get to the rehearsal. Few *basso* can cope with a long rehearsal, unable to eat enough they eventually turn yellow and faint. After about half an hour the rest of the band notice the *basso's* dilemma and drag him out of the rehearsal by his feet, down eight flights of stairs and chuck him out into the road where all too frequently they're run over by a 30 ton truck. Those that do survive eventually crawl back to join the rehearsal just in time to help the drummer pack away. Despite their tough existence *basso* will never moan or complain - well not much - at least not until drunk. Alcohol is very dangerous for *Basso* as only a few pints will ensure that anyone in earshot will be subjected to their wretched life story for hours.

BREEDING

Males and females of the species are both plentiful and it should be possible for the breed to remain pure. However, both male and female find themselves drawn to other species who seem to enjoy their tales of woe (unlike their own species). Union between *Basso* and *Vocalis* is extremely common.

WHERE IT IS FOUND

Usually down the pub at night and wandering parks and open spaces by day. These shy solitary creatures are generally easy to approach and totally harmless.

Basso simplex metalmoronus - **The Heavy Bass Player**

Easily identified by their sloping foreheads and long muscular arms. It is thought that *metalmoronus* is the result of cross-breeding between captured *basso complex* and chimpanzees.

Their instinct is to play bass but as they have the brain of a slightly cunning chimpanzee, all they can do is play the same note faster and faster. They can change note but only when prompted by the drummer ramming a drum stick up their anatomy. Without this prompt they'd never bother to play more than one note.

They are extremely useful to young bands starting out on the road. The combination of great stupidity and great strength means that they are great at carrying equipment around. With the right inducement - usually vodka - they'll clear the stage and pack the van in minutes, saving the band time and roadies fees.

Basso simplex completelybraindeadus - The Totally Crap Bass Player

Similar to *metalmoronus* in appearance and habit, *completelybraindeadus* has evolved from the original cross-breed into a virtual shell with very little resemblance to *homo sapiens* (remember all *musica* and *submusica* evolved originally from *sapiens*). Both males and females abound in quite large numbers. They frequently try to mate but fortunately are completely sterile.

They differ from *metalmoronus* on a practical level by being unable to play in time and don't have the speed of *metalmoronus* to hide how bad they are. Their best defence of this is to move their left hand around aimlessly so that the pitch is constantly changing. This creates as much racket as *metalmoronus* and is ideally suited to indie and punky styles.

Basso simplex steadyasarockus - **The Simple Rock Bass Player**

Simplex steadyasarockus is probably the most popular of all *Basso* with other *Musica* and *submusica* species. If you want root notes played together with the drummers kick, or in constant note patterns, *steadyasarockus* is there.

Essentially a thinking *metalmoronus* although the evolutionary path from chimpanzees, through *metalmoronus* is clear to see. Physically the species is spectacular. Both male and female are athletic and strong with only their rather long arms giving the game away.

They do suffer from dribbling at the mouth however and serious rock n rollers with a major drug problem find it impossible to hide this affliction. They can also be distinguished from *Basso complex* by their awkward body movement. There is no subtlety whatsoever. Don't propose a toast with them unless you want to be showered with drink and flying glass from the exploding glasses.

Although many *steadyasarockus* have a successful career, if they find the right band, most are destined to spend their time gigging in dives and out of the way pubs, where they find themselves being unfairly scrutinised by others of their species who haven't got a gig that night.

Basso complex thumbwaccus - The Slap Style Bass Player

Thumbwaccus recently evolved after a spate of marriages between female *drummus gadgetasaurus* and various *Basso complex* species.

Their offspring, whilst musically skilled are in fact totally mad. Easily recognised by their short cropped hair and deep set, pointy eyes that stare at you with that "no one's at home" kind of look.

Having a mother constantly tapping their heads and anything else, has led them to develop a very specific style of bass playing where they hit, rather than play the bass - effectively playing drums on the bass. Using their thumb to club the instrument repeatedly, while their left hand taps and whacks the fingerboard. They do, of course, need specially reinforced instruments made of toughened steel or carbon fibre.

Their stage presence is equally remarkable. They jump everywhere. Seriously hyperactive they'll jump all night - onto drum kits, monitors and in extreme cases onto the audience. Many are so dangerous in this 'gigging' state that they must be leashed or caged whilst on stage to prevent serious injury to themselves and members of the general public.

Now a rare sight, due to the excesses of some of the breed. Many are refused licences to gig and so have retreated to small obscure towns where they can play illegally.

Basso complex deus - The Great Bass Player

B. complex deus is in all probability from a totally different planet. Constantly sending messages to the mortals below. Certainly you'd think this, given the amount of hero worship they receive from others of their species.

Always busy, they are almost never seen in public, gliding unnoticed from studio to studio. Many now believe that the top few *Basso complex* are actually the same *Basso*. This has led some to believe in only one *complex deus*. This is beginning to split the *Basso simplex* family further from *Basso complex*, who believe in many gods.

B. complex deus is not in fact one *Basso complex* but the name given to all *Basso complex* capable of performing all types of *Basso* function. It is simply the case that only a few individuals of the basso species are capable of performing all styles and techniques.

Basso complex woodenboxus - The Upright Jazz Bass Player

Complex woodenboxus is named somewhat prophetically. His music is based around his huge wooden box of an instrument. The demands of playing and lugging around such a huge instrument takes its toll physically. Mentally the stress of having to deal with species like *Drummus technosmartarsus*, *Ivorytinklus beardex pseudointelectulus* and *Gitus ooharntaecleverus* would be enough to turn any species into a drug taking alcoholic. *Woodenboxus* is especially prone to take this road.

Easily identified, even without their instrument, as they are clearly descended from the pure bred bassos of ancient times but even as young as 22 they'll

look more like they're 45 and at 45 they're dead.

Fortunately for a species that is destined to die young the funeral costs are extremely low, just tuck them into their wooden bass, find a river and push - it's that simple. This is just as well as they are destined to die poverty stricken - even if they make money in their career, which is unlikely, they will always spend more than they earn.

ORIGIN

Ivorytinklus are a relatively modern phenomenon. There is only evidence for about 800 years of *Ivorytinklus*. The first *Ivorytinklus* would have come from *Homo sapiens*' cast-offs. For example those members of the clergy who were caught with their cassocks down and expelled would have drifted into keyboard playing. School teachers guilty of ravaging their young charges would again, on expulsion, gravitate towards keyboard playing. The habits and appearance of the modern *Ivorytinklus* can be traced back to these disgraced intellectuals and explains why they are usually either bald or bearded.

SIZE and GENERAL ANATOMY

Ivorytinklus is a very mixed breed and so can be almost any size but is mostly either bald (*Ivorytinklus baldus*) or bearded (*Ivorytinklus beardex pseudointelectulus*). Both are pseudo intellectual and both are gits. Many species are still very dangerous to young children, probably this is hereditary.

Although they have the largest brains of all *musica* species, only a few breeds such as *I. Baldus intelectulus* actually use their brains in an intellectual way. Mostly their minds simply operate overtime on working out how to progress their own career at the expense of every other species.

HABITAT

The natural habitat of *Ivorytinklus* is amongst *Homo sapiens*. Being a recent evolution from diseased members of society they have no historic origin or habitat.

HABITS

The main habit of *Ivorytinklus* is to bullshit everyone. Of course, to do this well they must study music to some degree. Their aim is to convince their circle of musician friends that they are massive musical intellects. They know more about music than anyone else, they will always try to tell other species how to play their own instrument. They'll always be the first to moan if anyone is even thinking about going out of tune. Generally their aim is to take over any band they join and, in their sad little minds at least, to eventually take over the world. They are always brilliant song writers able to write a hit in ten minutes, if only they could be bothered.

FOOD

Lots and lots of food. Because of the vast amount of brain power that goes into every intellectual moment of playing any type of keyboard, several tons of sausage, egg and chips are required 3 times a day. Well, this is what keyboard players would have us believe. The truth is they're all fat greedy bastards to a man (or woman) and will eat anything so long as there's sufficient quantity on hand.

BREEDING

The origin of *Ivorytinklus* gives a clue as to why the female of the species is less common. Originally, because only males had intellectual jobs from which they could be expelled meant there were no females to be found in nature. The excessive lust, natural to

all *Ivorytinklus* meant that they never had a problem being attracted to all other species. The only problem was would the other species be attracted to them, being either bald or bearded. The answer was no. *Ivorytinklus* got around the problem of a mate by forming small music groups. The group would gather in the late afternoon and seek out a small crowd, such as at a bus stop. Initially they wait patiently eyeing up the group (usually young *sapiens*). Eventually they would pick out the weakest member of the group

and then gradually close in, worrying the group into dispersing and isolating the weakest member of the group.

Once captured the helpless *sapiens* would be subjected to unmentionable things by one or all of the *Ivorytinklus* involved. Eventually completely embarrassed by their ordeal, they'd be forced into marrying one of them and bearing many children in the hope that one might be annoying enough to one day become a great keyboard player, just like his or her dad.

WHERE IT IS FOUND

Widely dispersed, *Ivorytinklus* seems to thrive on the company of *Homo sapiens*. This is probably because by trying to train *sapiens* to become musical they have a constant supply of ignorant people who they can impress with their musical knowledge.

There is such a huge variety of species that one type or another is present in almost every village, town or city.

Ivorytinklus pubus - The Common Pub Keyboard Player

Ivorytinklus pubus has increased in numbers alarmingly over the past two decades. Encouraged by cheap keyboard equipment and advancing technology in anti spot creams, they can be found in almost any pub entertainment situation.

Unusually for *Ivorytinklus*, *pubus* is neither bald nor bearded. This has led some experts to call for a re-classification, believing that *pubus* is not a true *Ivorytinklus*.

Whatever the outcome of this argument the rest of us have to daily endure these over enthusiastic prats. They are never highly skilled keyboard players being content to carelessly hit chord after chord believing that this might be good enough to convince us they're playing the song intended. They certainly have no concept of arrangement and take little notice of the band. It is this final point that convinces me that *pubus* is a genuine *Ivorytinklus*.

They generally get on well with *Vocalis* and *Drummus* (both *submusica*) but are never happy when talking to *Gitus* and *Basso*. This is in sharp contrast to other *Ivorytinklus* who delight in showing that they're better than their other *musica* cousins. Their insistence on playing and hogging all the bass lines brings them into constant conflict with *Basso simplex*. Were it not for the placid nature of *Basso*, it is highly likely that *Ivorytinklus pubus* would have the crap beaten out of him daily (there's no justice in the world).

Ivorytinklus cantplaysomakesillynoisesonasynthus - **The Synth Player**

The ridiculously but aptly named *cantplaysomakesillynoisesonasynthus* is, like *pubus*, of questionable origin and should possibly be re-classified. The argument for remaining classified *Ivorytinklus* is again made because of their amazing talent for ignoring all other musicians.

There must surely be some *Vocalis Grand prattus* blood in them from somewhere as they are easily the most vain of all *Ivorytinklus*. The vanity is different from *Prattus giganticus* in that *giganticus* simply believes he (or she) is some kind of god so the vanity is inside. *Cantplaysomakesilly-noisesonasynthus* on the other hand, is obsessed with looks. Unlike any other *Ivorytinklus* they'll spend hours in front of a mirror making up and creating stupid hairdos. They must dress in outrageous clothes, the males preferring women's clothing and the females dress as men. All of the preening is to disguise how bad they are. They can enhance this disguise by buying loads of really expensive equipment. This, like all types of financial inducement, makes them really popular with the other musicians - this and their drug sourcing connections anyway.

Ivorytinklus baldus intelectulus - The Classical Pianist

Baldus intelectulus considers himself at the top of the musical food chain (or herself as there are many females that are classified baldus - characterised by a high hair line and hardly any eyebrows).

Completely wrapped up in their own self-importance they glide into studios and concert halls around the globe. They are bald at birth, through childhood and till death and so their parents have no choice other than to prepare them for a life on the concert stage.

Of course, they must still study hard. Simply being bald is not enough. The only problem is that they forget to mix with others or have any sort of normal life whatsoever. This makes them extremely unpredictable as characters. Sometimes extremely charming and gracious but able to change instantly into a ranting, raving lunatic. Many go completely mad, although this is often helpful to their career.

In order to command an audience and hold their attention, *Baldus intelectulus* must not only master the music, but also severe and completely over the top arm movements and facial expressions.

Ivorytinklus playalongus - The Pub Play-Along Pianist

I.playalongus was essentially a common breed brought about by introducing female *Vocalis pututosleepus* to *Ivorytinklus baldus intelectulus*. Not you might imagine a match made in heaven but actually a very accommodating relationship, *pututosleepus* being able to easily subdue the over-stressed *baldus* enabling them to relax for the first time.

The result is a promising *Ivorytinklus* when young that will gradually come under the mother *V. pututosleepus's* influence. This moves them away from classical study into playing first rag time songs and then gradually they get simpler and simpler until they're playing standards. The problem gets worse as they find they can make easy money for doing, what for them, is no work.

Always seriously overweight, *I. playalongus* is jolly by nature and ideally suited to playing for *sapiens* to try and sing along with. As they get older they get fatter and fatter until a very messy explosion takes place.

The breed is now quite rare as most pubs have alternative forms of entertainment. Also marriages between *Vocalis pututosleepus* to *Ivorytinklus baldus intelectulus* are now quite rare.

So far no conservation groups have stepped forward to try and save the breed, most people apparently quite happy to see the back of them.

I'd like to see a small working farm established to protect this rare and less popular breed from vanishing altogether. That way we could drag them out of obscurity on the odd occasions we need a silly song about football or snooker but are otherwise not bothered by them.

Ivorytinklus beardex pseudointelectulus - **The Bearded Pianist**

I. beardex pseudointelectulus is an interesting phenomenon of modern times. Extremely studious when young, their primary characteristic only comes to light when the beard is fully developed. This is the urge to abandon their classical upbringing and take to the rock stage. It doesn't matter where or when, large or small, as long as they can join in with a real pop or rock band.

At first, other band members are enthusiastic, almost honoured that such a highly qualified *musica* should want to join their humble band. What they don't realise is that ever so slowly, *I. beardex pseudointelectulus* will monopolise every aspect of the band. They use their knowledge of chords and keys to completely baffle all weaker species of *musica* and *submusica*. Their influence over *drummus* is limited as it simply goes in one ear and out of the other.

Poor *basso simplex* is completely overwhelmed with only pure bred *Basso complex* being able to withstand the onslaught. *I. beardex pseudointelectulus* can simply introduce a *Basso* to so many new

concepts for creating bass lines that he cannot cope on his own any more.

You would imagine that *I. beardex pseudointelectulus* would come into conflict with *Gitus* in a big way. Not so, as *I. beardex pseudointelectulus* is extremely cunning. Luring *Gitus* into playing harmonised solos *I. beardex pseudointelectulus* can use *Gitus'* emotion to steal the limelight himself. *Gitus* is too wrapped up in his own ego to realise of course.

On stage they, of course, look like complete prats and so stack up multiple keyboards to hide behind. They then dress up in long sleeved costumes which can enhance their pose. When on stage *I. beardex pseudointelectulus* is somewhere between *I. baldus intelectulus* and *I. prattus giganticus*.

The problem for this breed is that as they get older they become trapped by their beard. Unable to shave (this would be fatal) they cannot miraculously evolve into *I. baldus intelectulus* which is who they'd like to be when older. They cannot forcibly become *I. prattus giganticus* either because that sort of insanity must be genetic. So after taking a break from rock and pop bands they eventually drift back into playing old fashioned rock and pop music.

They are often found on cruise ships where their natural ability to ignore everyone is perfectly suited. They find that they naturally fit the role of Musical Director and it is now known that musical directors are not a separate species but simply *I. beardex pseudointelectulus* over 35 years of age.

I. beardex pseudointelectulus will change with the role. Whereas the young *I. beardex pseudointelectulus* is quite well liked at first by bands that he or she joins, by the time they turn into musical directors they will be liked by no one. In the vicious world or *musica* and *submusica* they are then entering a dangerous world where they must take their personal security very seriously as almost everyone will want them dead.

Such is the hatred they inspire that many are slaughtered while they sit at the piano. Any method of ridding the world of these creeps is OK. The only complaint is from the floor manager of the ship or function room, who's got to clear away the mess.

Ivorytinklus prattus giganticus - Too Good To Need Anyone Else

I. prattus giganticus is like *I. beardex pseudointelectulus* gone mad. They become totally obsessed with themselves. This self adulation carries on into their playing. Having taken over many bands and caused their destruction, *I. prattus giganticus* can only take to the stage alone. Their ego has become so large that they think they can play to hundreds of thousands of people without any other person visible on stage. Worse still, they believe that the audience will actually enjoy the show if it lasts several hours.

The police will tell a different story, as frequently they have to clear stadiums of the corpses of multiple suicides. These unfortunate *sapiens*, believing that they're going to see the keyboard player from their former favourite band - perhaps even a few songs that they know - are instead treated to an evening of such self-indulgence that few can survive without major trauma. Chords can sometimes be held for over an hour without changing, as *prattus giganticus* slowly waves his free hand up and down to an over elaborate light show.

In severe cases, *I. prattus giganticus* may have several sequencers that are triggered, one at a time while *giganticus* prances about the stage to a layer of musical nonsense.

Some *I. prattus giganticus* have 'light harps' on stage so that they can make a huge show out of 'plucking' this beam of light. They 'pluck', a silly noise comes out - initially the audience cheer. Now drunk with adulation from the naive crowd, *I. prattus giganticus* plucks again. Again more cheers - I suppose we deserve it really.

Let's face it, whatever talent they might once have had, by the time *I. prattus giganticus* matures they are no better than Karaoke singers. Totally reliant on a pre-composed and recorded backing tracks. The only difference is that *I. prattus giganticus* doesn't even have to speak. He can spend all evening bathing in spot lights, throwing back his thick, long hair and playing about as much keyboards as *I. cantplaysomakesillynoisesonasynthus*.

ORIGIN

Evidence of *Blowjobus* goes back thousands of years. Probably as early as when people first started putting things in their mouths and blowing they realised that silly noises could be made. From here it was constant development, although the principle of the modern wind instrument remains the same - a pipe with holes in it.

Modern *blowjobus* has evolved into a number of sub-species along with a variety of instruments although all *blowjobus* share the following characteristics. Where a species differs from the rest will be made clear in each section.

SIZE and GENERAL ANATOMY

A young *blowjobus* is easily spotted in infancy. Every object is put to the mouth to see if it makes a noise when blowed. (This is distinctly different to brass players who will use only their lips to make silly noises - even when adult.)

At about 4 years of age the different physiological differences that will determine whether *blowjobus* will be *tongus*, *lipus*, *nonlipusmaximus*, or *saxus*.

Tongus; can be difficult to spot at an early age as it's not the size of the tongue that's different but the speed and complexity of movement that it can naturally achieve. Once identified a young *tongus*

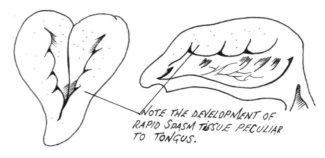

NOTE THE DEVELOPMENT OF RAPID SPASM TISSUE PECULIAR TO TONGUS.

will be given a flute to practise

Lipus; develops fleshy lips capable of withstanding severe vibration for long periods of time. These begin to develop at about 6 years of age. *Lipus* youngsters will usually be given a clarinet to play.

Nonlipusmaximus; from about the age of 4 first the upper lip and soon after the lower lip begin to disappear into the mouth. By puberty the lips have disappeared altogether and as a result huge fleshy

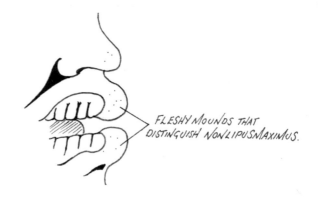

FLESHY MOUNDS THAT DISTINGUISH NONLIPUSMAXIMUS.

mounds appear where the lips should be - this gives *nonlipusmaximus* great strength to grasp the small bony oboe or cor anglais reed firmly and blow.

Saxus; a recently evolved sub-species, *saxus* is really a mutation of *Lipus*.

HABITAT

Generally found in leafy middle class suburbs with the exception of *blowjobus saxus* which differs from the rest of *blowjobus* by preferring ghettos and shacks in the centre of large cities. Although all *blowjobus* are nocturnal to some extent, most go to bed early except for *saxus* who must stay awake till dawn when its finally time to sleep.

HABITS

Most *blowjobus* are disciplined and practise their instruments at the same time daily except for Monday when they do their laundry and clean themselves in preparation for a week of auditions. This is because *blowjobus* are rarely permanently employed.

The habits of *blowjobus saxus* are different from others of the species in that they don't really bother with the laundry.

FOOD

Almost any food so long as it's liquid or mashed up finely. *Blowjobus* can only feed by reversing their natural blowing instincts into sucking. They are rarely invited to dinner as a result - imagine the noise - embarrassing or what!

BREEDING

Breeding stock is still quite pure, although with the recent mutation of *blowjobus lipus* into *blowjobus saxus* the likelihood of inter-breeding with *Homo sapiens* has increased. This is especially true of female *blowjobus saxus* - no doubt the suggestive nature of their playing habits having something to do with it.

WHERE IT IS FOUND

Widely dispersed in Western Europe, America and Russia there are small pockets found in the far east in China and Japan. America has the highest concentration of *saxus* anywhere in the world where there are an estimated 250,000 roaming wild in big city parks.

The more refined breeds tend to stick to the suburbs where they shuffle quietly back and forth from their quiet little flats situated in expensive areas hoping that no one realises that they only have a tiny flat amongst all the big, flash houses.

B. saxus anaesthetisus - The Elevator Music Sax Player

Anaesthetisus is sadly becoming more and more widespread. Originally bred to help counter stress in *Homo sapiens*. Unfortunately, after their introduction from America into Europe the species has simply run riot with every *Blowjobus* on the planet pretending they too can play smooth soulful jazz.

Of course, in the right environment their music can be genuinely therapeutic - rest homes, hospices etc.. However, in a live theatre or hall these creatures can be deadly - some of the audience falling so deeply asleep that they have been pronounced dead at the scene.

Males and females are found in roughly equal numbers although the two rarely meet. As the breed is fairly new it is as yet unknown whether offspring from male and female *anaesthetisus* would be born alive or completely sound asleep unable to ever wake up. Let's hope we never find out.

The problems associated with an over-population of *anaesthetisus* are made worse by their inevitable associations with other similar breeds such as *vocalis pututosleepus* and *drummus technosmartarsus*. Often *Ivorytinklus* and the related *Raspberryblowus trumpetae whathehellnoteisthatus*. When all of the above form a band and gig, the devastation is total and, should sound escape from the hall can even affect passing motorists with often fatal consequences.

B. saxus selfdestructus - The Great Doomed Sax Player

For *Selfdestructus*, like so many of the *musica* species that are tempted to find fulfilment playing jazz, life is destined to be hard. Exploitation is almost guaranteed. Their life revolves around playing down a metal tube. They know nothing of how the world works and so must rely on others to guide them through the world of showbiz and life - whoops, big mistake!

Once *submusica hangersonus* has his claws into a *selfdestructus* the pattern is clear. Feeding *selfdestructus* just enough to live on and distracting them in their leisure time by laying on women, drugs and alcohol, *selfdestructus* never has a chance. They believe all the time that their talent will save them and so practise constantly to achieve greatness. Sometimes this greatness is recognised widely and their agent will make a lot of money and sometimes not.

The outcome is sadly always the same. *Selfdestructus* eventually sees the world for what it is and decides to stop and get off. Who can blame them for seeking everlasting peace and quiet after a lifetime of jazz.

B. saxus squeakypubus - The Crap Sax Player

All species have a cousin they'd rather not acknowledge. *Squeakypubus* is one such example. Although they start off promisingly and have the same breeding roots as *selfdestructus* and *anaesthetisus* they get distracted during and after adolescence by the opposite sex. Males of the species are especially led astray when they start teaching girls how to blow their pipe.

This gap in their training and upbringing is devastating. Instead of finding themselves being sought after by anyone who's anyone, they struggle even to get into a crappy pub band or badly paid function band.

Unfortunately for mankind we'd rather they didn't manage to get into any band at all. Poor tone is bad enough but when they miss a note and squeak we all suffer dreadfully.

Squeakypubus is very aware of the pain that is caused by this phenomenon and becomes totally paranoid. They play with their eyes on the escape door and the quickest route out in case someone turns nasty. This is rare because the damage done to most eardrums by a squeaky sax player takes it out of even the most violent audience. If *squeakypubus* is having an especially bad night then they are in real danger of a lynching - by the rest of the band.

B. *nonlipusmaximus* - Oboe Player

Nonlipusmaximus find that their physical disability of having no lips makes them easy targets for other species. Thus, they keep themselves to themselves.

There are many instruments that they can adapt themselves to; Oboe, Cor Anglais, Bassoon, Shehnai and Nadaswaram. They are easily confused about which instrument they're playing with often disastrous results for the snake they're trying to charm.

B. *tongus* - The Flute Player

Both males and females are voracious and popular lovers. No other species can match their complex tongue movements. They can adapt themselves to flute or piccolo and can often play many other instruments of their greater species.

Recently there has been an increase in *B. tongus anaesthetisus*. Playing mind-blowingly bland music for easy money has been a constant temptation for *B. tongus* for many years.

ORIGIN

Raspberryblowus, like *blowjobus* have been slowly evolving for thousands of years. From the moment the first human blew a raspberry to insult another, brass players were only just around the corner.

However, the first *raspberryblowus* had to wait until metal was invented before they could expand their musical repertoire into anything more than a silly rude noise.

As soon as the first metal pipe was invented there were *raspberryblowus*. Early brass players were extremely important to armies who made use of their high pitched loud sound to pass instruction across a battlefield.

SIZE and GENERAL ANATOMY

Generally quite a large creature they have evolved especially large lungs. They can also breathe in through their nose while exhaling through their mouth. They are the only species known to be able to do this. Many have evolved lung tissue in their cheeks which further expands their ability to store air and propel it out of their mouths at high speed. Their lips and tongue are specially adapted to be brought together in that sort of pout so useful for raspberry blowing. They are constantly evolving. More than any other species they are changing physically. As with all forms of evolution as soon as a *raspberryblowus* is successful and therefore ready to breed, any

characteristics developed uniquely will be passed on to the next generation and so on.

HABITAT

Found almost anywhere the rest of us aren't. Because of the racket they make they are shunned by society and banished to derelict military housing estates where they accelerate the demolition process by practising for hours on end.

They occasionally stray into the big cities when they've got a job playing a TV theme or teaming up with *Blowjobus saxus* to create a pop brass section.

HABITS

Playful creatures, even in adulthood they chase each other around the deserted streets playing 'raspberry'. A bit like paint ball, except with spit. Generally dedicated creatures they spend many hours practising. Many are naturally experimental and because they can play strange notes that don't belong to any other species scales, they do. Many do this accidentally, others seduced by the seedy world of jazz play these notes intentionally, constantly confusing and delighting other musica by their ability to get away with playing almost any note they feel like.

FOOD

Raspberryblowus need carbohydrates in massive quantities. The sheer physical demands of pouting and blowing raspberries all day requires them to attend to their diet. Pasta is a real favourite. Spaghetti in particular can be slurped up using their natural pout. If you're ever caught in an Italian restaurant next to a table of *Raspberryblowus*, either move tables or ask that a shower curtain be erected between your table and the *Raspberryblowus* table.

BREEDING

Females are much less common than the males and as is so common in this situation getting *Raspberryblowus* to remain pure bred is very difficult. In Roman times their masters would ensure that they only ever mated with their own kind. Today, *sapiens*

is fascinated by the idea of strong, pouting vibrating lips. So, even though *Raspberryblowus* may want to be true to his kind he is all too often seduced by drunken *sapiens*.

WHERE IT IS FOUND

Although not found in large numbers anywhere, *Raspberryblowus* can be found in and around most towns and cities. They must live outside of town, away from others and do their practise outside of built up areas but they will descend on the towns and cities in quite large numbers once night has fallen.

Their homes are only sparsely decorated due to the inevitable damage caused by practising their craft. Many *Raspberryblowus* will marry their own kind and raise pure *Raspberryblowus*. Their homes need to be specially constructed of concrete and built to much the same specification as homes built in earthquake zones. As yet no one has dared film or study a pure bred family of *Raspberryblowus* as it would be extremely dangerous for any other species to get close.

My studies brought me on many occasions to within a few hundred yards of such families but the noise and risk of falling masonry proved simply too dangerous to get in really close.

Trumpetae whathehellnoteisthatus - The Jazz Trumpet Player

Trumpetae whathehellnoteisthatus has existed since the dawn of the instrument itself. For thousands of years this breed was shunned by *musica* species for being complete crap. However, with the arrival of the 20th century this species suddenly found that the strange notes that through all previous forms of music were simply out of tune, or the wrong note now worked. It was incredible, like a blind man seeing for the first time these creatures could stand up on stage and be heroes. They were of course playing jazz.

Even today no other instrumental species of *musica* can get away with the peculiar pitches and melodies of the jazz trumpeter.

As the species grew in popularity various sub species developed such as *whathehellmutus* who've evolved by putting strange shaped objects over the bell of their instrument to change the sound.

Trumpetae highnoteobsessivus - **The Overloud Trumpet Player**

Trumpetae highnoteobsessivus is one of the oldest of all species of *musica*. Like most ancient species their use to *Homo sapiens* was within the military. This species was specially bred to hit higher and higher notes. To play louder and louder. The uses to the military leaders in Roman times and before was immense.

Not only could communications be made across battlefields but also stone and glass could be shattered from great distances. Any *Homo sapiens* within earshot could be annoyed and deafened to death.

Today they are the show-offs in the world of *Raspberry-blowus*. They insist on demonstrating at every turn their highest, loudest most piercing note. Their one big advantage in the modern world is that they need no amplification even within the context of a loud Latin ensemble.

In South America, where the species is not only tolerated but actually revered by most other species, large numbers of *highnoteobsessivus* may be present in the same band. Often they will add flashy technique and super fast playing to their natural skill of being really loud and annoying. The species is less w e l l tolerated in Europe where they are banned from urban centres unless they have a pass to play a TV theme or some other type of session.

ORIGIN

Screechus, whilst not as ancient as *drummus* and *blowjobus* species are nevertheless a very old species. String instruments evolved from early attempts to make different grades of rope from the guts of lesser species. *Screechus'* ancestors noticed that by plucking or dragging an archery bow across the tightly drawn rope, that a strange noise could be produced. Eventually sound boxes were crafted that would amplify the sound and from here the different sub species evolved; *violinii*, *violus*, *cellae* and *doublebasso*.

SIZE and GENERAL ANATOMY

The males are not especially tall but make up for this by being stocky. They have almost as large a brain as *Ivorytinklus* but emotionally are much more powerful. Females are often very severe, strong creatures but about one in fifty will be very, very pretty (see *tooprettytobeseriousae* on page 71). Their eyes are always close together from their long evolution of looking straight down their nose at their instrument. Their hair is always big - no real evolutionary reason for this, it's just always been that way.

HABITAT

A quiet species, *screechus* need to be especially careful with their young. This is because the young

screechus is completely intolerable to any other species, and if heard before a mature sound has developed, would be hunted down and killed by almost every species on the planet.

This has led *screechus* to adopt a nomadic way of life, coming into the cities in time for the Proms and other cultural events. Having been emotionally charged they trek out to country regions to breed. Before the females grow too heavy with child, *screechus* must make its way to the equatorial deserts and away, a long way away, from all other living species. Here they must stay, training their young to produce a good tone before daring to return to civilization.

HABITS

Extremely dedicated to their species and their craft, most *screechus* will practise for hours and hours, initially in the desperate search for a good tone, and as they master this they search for perfect emotional content. A *screechus* that cannot induce tears in it's audience by the time it's 12 or 13 is unlikely to ever become a serious soloist and will by then be resigned to orchestral playing. Some *screechus* are ostracised by their own kind when they either begin playing on pop records or worse still, playing electric violin. Any suggestion of amplifying the violin in particular is frowned upon by the elders who remember only to well the persecution they've suffered from purely acoustic playing. Their fear is justified as frequently the type of *screechus* that's seduced into the world of electronics will be a screechus that would otherwise end up in the 3rd violins of a small provincial orchestra. This means a real danger that other species might hear really bad string playing and lash out at all *screechus* setting the species back hundreds of years in it's quest for acceptance.

FOOD

They are not usually big eaters, what they do eat is usually delicately spiced and eaten with rice or simple breads. The pure bred, traditional *screechus* rarely drink more than an occasional glass of wine and then only if the wine is an excellent vintage. Modern drugs are frowned upon and would only be taken by outcast *screechus*.

They do have one unfortunate habit, brought about no doubt by their upbringing in the desert. Large insects are a delicacy. They find a butterfly or beetle irresistible and if one should rather stupidly land near their picnic table they'll be snatched up and eaten in the blink of an eye. This can be quite embarrassing in polite society and can land *screechus* in big trouble should it happen at some really hoity toity do.

BREEDING

Cross-breeding with other species is outlawed in *screechus* society. Only those *screechus* that have become outcasts would consider shacking up with another species. Little is known about the resulting offspring from a *screechus* cross-breeding. It is likely though that the youngster would be set upon and killed if he or she ever started trying to learn to play within earshot of other species.

WHERE IT IS FOUND

Screechus is only ever found on the well worn nomadic trails. These exist between most of the large deserts of the world and the nearest big city to them. Obviously the modern world has produced the phenomenon of the star *screechus* and these stars would of course have to travel the world away from their own community for many months at a time. *Screechus* that achieve star status generally adapt well to being away from their family and community and of course are revered by all other species and so are quite safe.

Outcast *screechus* are in danger at all times. Many get drunk and not realising that they are living within earshot of all other species in a big town or city begin trying to play. They are bad enough at the best of times and in their drunken state would be intolerable. As it's still not a crime to slay undeveloped or outcast *screechus*, many are simply slaughtered and dumped.

Violinii wailingwallus- The Israeli Violinist

As with all young *screechus*, *wailingwallus* is born in the desert miles from civilisation. Here they must quickly learn the art of playing the violin. The faster they learn the quicker they can leave the desert. *Wailingwallus* is told this story a thousand times already, by parents and grandparents, aunts and uncles. Studying hard to develop technique and tone *wailingwallus* is usually ready to join mainstream society by the age of 7 or 8 years old. (Most *screechus* will be in their teens before this is possible.)

Their early life reflects the history of their religion. They soon learn that by using the pain of generations their violin playing advances rapidly. Not only does it help their playing but also the tearful reaction of their first audiences further encourages them to learn more about their history which makes their playing still more emotional and so it goes on.

By the time they are in their early teens ordinary *sapiens* at the concert hall have no defence against the emotional playing of *wailingwallus* and will cry unashamedly at the poignancy and beauty of the music. Modern concert halls are built to take the vast amount of salt water that pours down the aisles but some early *wailingwallus* were simply swept away by a tidal wave of grief.

Wailingwallus can live to be well over one hundred and fifty years old, provided they don't get political, which would mean certain assassination. They'll insist on giving concerts right up to the time they're being carted away in a wooden box.

Funerals are attended by generations of *wailingwallus*, all of whom will play pieces from the dead *wailingwallus'* repertoire.

Violinii tooprettytobeseriousae - **The Pretty Violinist**

All *screechus* species are brought up in desolate surroundings. As they're growing up females of the species are completely unaware of whether they're attractive or not. This means that in common with their species they natu- rally work hard to escape their harsh sur- roundings.

It is only on arrival at the big cities that they slowly become aware of their looks. The frumpy ones go on to be successful concert violinists or orchestral players. The terribly pretty ones soon realise that there is big money to be made by simply playing violin in a skimpy dress. The more flesh they expose the bigger the fee. In extreme cases some will even

consider playing along to a hip-hop backing track and head into the world of pop music. For some the rewards can be huge either as a solo artist or by joining a band as backing vocalist and occasional violinist. Obviously in either case the main objective is to stand there and look pretty. For some reason this is a real turn on for *sapiens* to see a former classical player half naked playing a Beethoven concerto backed by bass and drums.

ORIGIN

Hititus, which include conga and bongo players, are descendants of early *drummus*. When *Drummus* was sweeping north from Africa in about 50 BC a large group became stranded from the main group. The island they found themselves marooned on was a paradise for the early *Drummus*. Filled with gourds, hollowed out tree stumps and large sea shells. So distracted was the separated group that they quickly forgot their fellow *drummus* (and who could blame them). Within a generation or so, almost every naturally occurring object on the island had been gathered and turned into a valid percussion instrument. Where an object didn't make a very good noise on its own it could be combined with other objects that could scrape or scratch the original object. Isolated for hundreds of years early *drummus* evolved slowly into a distinct species '*Hititus*'. Within this species two groups developed and generally, although at peace with one another, kept themselves separated. One group became obsessed with any object that made an interesting noise - we now call them percussionists (*Hititus annoyingus maximus*) - and those that wanted to preserve their *drummus* roots, who used the hollowed out tree trunks - we now call this group bongo and conga players (*Hititus thikckdrunkenbastus*).

SIZE and GENERAL ANATOMY

Physically much smaller than *Drummus*. They evolved into much smaller skinnier creatures than their distant cousins presumably because there were no predators in their tropical paradise. They are easily recognisable from their Hawaiian shirt patterned skin.

HABITAT

Although a totally tropical species until discovered in 1643, *Hititus* quickly established themselves in many cities - especially port cities. From here they gradually spread all over the place and are now regarded as pests by most other species.

HABITS

Hititus annoyingus maximus spend most of their time foraging for anything that makes an interesting noise. *Hititus thickcdrunkenbastus* have generally become victims of the modern world being seduced by whiskey and an easy gig.

FOOD

As long as there's coconut in it, they'll eat it. Curried turtle with coconut washed down by a bottle of Malibu will feed a *Hititus* for a week. Although most *Hititus* are hyperactive they still become addicted to cocaine which only adds to their manic reputation.

BREEDING

For a breed that was totally pure and isolated for centuries *Hititus* has become totally promiscuous and inter-bred. On their isolated island there were always strict controls on marriage and breeding. As soon as they found themselves exposed to the world at large something in them snapped and they shagged everybody.

There is now a concerted effort by conservationists to try and rescue the species. As males and females abound in roughly equal numbers this should be straightforward. However many are either gay or completely uninterested in their own kind, nor whether the species is preserved. By capturing and isolating a few specially chosen males and females it is hoped that this once fascinating species may yet be saved.

WHERE IT IS FOUND

Although many Hititus have tried to get back to their tropical roots by heading to the Caribbean and other tropical islands, *Hititus* is now found in all countries. In the developed world they typically prefer the big cities although many *Hititus thickcdrunkenbastus,* destroyed by their dependence on alcohol, find themselves in small towns and villages joining a young unsuspecting band as the conga player. Here they manage a few songs before collapsing in a drunken heap, occasionally crawling back to their congas to add a token beat in the specially composed quiet bit.

Hititus is rarely wealthy. They'd only spend the money on stupid bits of percussion anyway. They would seek out simple shelter in their wild tropical paradise and so long as they can keep warm they need little in the way of luxuries.

Many *Hititus thickcdrunkenbastus* have no concept of where they live. Typically they'll sleep where they drop and get up when they're moved on. So bad is the situation in many cities that forced repatriation to any tropical island that will take them is now a common policy.

Hititus annoyingus maximus- The Totally Annoying Percussionist

Annoyingus maximus is one of the commonest of all *Hititus*. Whereever they are they just have to hit everything to see if it can be used in their percussion set up. Whether rich or poor, successful or not all *annoyingus maximus* will have a huge set up. They have every gadget imaginable, tambourines and timbales are of course part of the set up but they'll also have sticks, shells, stupid rows of metal pipes called strangely 'bell trees'. Other favourites are vibra-slaps, a hundred assorted cowbells, claves, saws and bits that go boing.

Once established in a band they are hard to shift. All bands go through a phase where they believe a percussionist will help them become really exotic only to realise too late that these annoying bastards make noises the whole time.

This is really their downfall - if only they could control themselves and play when it was really needed then they could be useful members of musical society.

However, they're always entertaining to watch and if you can find ways of controlling them (opiates are quite effective) then they can be useful band members.

Hititus thickdrunkenbastus - **The Bongo Player**

All families of animals have a species at the bottom of the food chain. At the bottom of the musical food chain lies the *Hititus thickdrunkenbastus*.

A true *Hititus thickdrunkenbastus* is pure bred but is easily mistaken for an aging *drummus*. There's very little difference. Both have pretty much lost the will to live. They need an instrument that can be played in the background in almost every musical situation. They need to be able to stagger home with their instrument tucked under one arm and

they need to be able to do no work whatsoever.

You may think why do bands allow them to join in but *musica* are naturally caring creatures and feel that they need to help those less fortunate and talented than themselves.

ORIGIN

As soon as the *musica* and *submusica* species began to evolve differently from the rest of *Homo sapiens* it was inevitable that some would further evolve to take advantage of the newly evolving species. *Hangersonus insidious* and *Hangersonus fleecus* are two of the most ancient of these species. Feeding quite literally on all other species

SIZE and GENERAL ANATOMY

Physically repulsive, these creatures have developed green blood. Up close, it is possible to see that their skin is actually made up of small scales. The skin, like their minds is totally immune to any outside influence or infection. Both hands are extremely course and scaly with prominent claws, especially the female. Both male and female are identical in height and weight. They are naturally short and often seriously overweight.

Physically there is not much difference between *Hangersonus insidious* and *Hangersonus fleecus*. *Hangersonus fleecus* though does not have the long forked tongue of *Hangersonus insidious*. This gives him the edge over *insidious* in business because other species are fooled into thinking that they might be trustworthy whereas you know never to trust *Hangersonus insidius* just by looking at them. This is why *insidius* rarely gets the chance to do more than book artists for their 10% as opposed to *fleecus* who'll manage, usually for 25% or even 50% of *musica's* earnings.

HABITS

Both *insidious* and *fleecus* spend the morning asleep. They will get up in time to go to an expensive restaurant for a light breakfast when everyone else is eating lunch. They'll drop into their office about 3:00pm, not to do any work but so that they can slag off everyone who works for them, threatening them with the sack before being nice just long enough to stop them all walking out voluntarily.

At night, they do business. Poaching is their favourite pastime. They have no respect for others of

their kind and will poach another agent or manager's artist at any opportunity. They all drive around in the most expensive limo they can afford to hire, each trying to out do the other in an effort to persuade artists to sign to them. Once they've signed an artist they will do anything to protect them from others of their kind. If this means not booking any work for the artist then so be it - in the interests of the artist of course.

They fear no other creature except *Overpaedus* and *Bullshitus*, who they revere. If it were not a matter of breeding then all *Hangersonus* would become *Overpaedus*. They'll even get up in the morning if *Overpaedus* offers them a meeting. Usually *Overpaedus* is just taking the piss and will cancel the meeting quarter of an hour before it's due to begin, often hiding in reception to witness the spectacular display of *Hangersonus insidious* or *Hangersonus fleecus* spitting and cursing as they realise they've been tricked into getting up early.

FOOD

Blood. Not a lot else is needed - often they will eat whole creatures and will sometimes eat carrion if the star was famous enough. When they're not doing too well then they can survive for many months on an insect only diet.

BREEDING

Whenever they get the chance. They will breed with anyone sufficiently well drugged. However, the breed is one of the few where actual marriage and the production of pure bred *Hangersonus insidious* and *Hangersonus fleecus* is carefully maintained by a tightly knit community. They can only marry their own kind otherwise they'll become outcasts. Without the protection of the clan they would soon perish - set upon by someone they'd ripped off years before.

Their bastard offspring brought about by date rape of innocent *vocalis* etc. are one reason why some *musica* are evolving into crap musicians that can only progress by exploiting others.

WHERE IT IS FOUND

Anywhere there are species of *musica* and *submusica* they'll be a *Hangersonus insidious* and *Hangersonus fleecus* not far behind.

They tend to confine themselves to specific areas of large cities. This is partly so that they don't have to travel very far to do business and partly because they need the protection of their own community.

They'll always live beyond their means just about managing to cling onto a glitzy lifestyle. They will always prefer apartments to houses and they certainly have no use for gardens, preferring concrete and brick for surroundings. They will decorate their surroundings with shiny objects and will collect anything that looks expensive or antique from a distance.

ORIGIN

Because of the attention always afforded good musicians, it was inevitable that a group would evolve along side them that wished they could be musical but that had no talent. They had to develop skills and characteristics that would provide support for their talented cousins. Two species dominate *Technopissartisae*: *T. fatuselessgitus* and *T. fullofthemselvsus*.

In early times this would have meant carrying and cleaning instruments. In modern times their role can be quite sophisticated - it's not just gaffering cables to the floor you know - sometimes they've got to plug in the instruments as well.

SIZE and GENERAL ANATOMY

Both sub-species are similar anatomically. Large clumsy creatures, their resemblance to *Basso simplex metalmoronus* is uncanny at times, although there is little evidence that they are descended from *metalmoronus*.

They are more likely to be descendants of various *Hangersonus* species but it is extremely likely that an animal got in there at some time - probably gorilla.

Arms and legs are very primate but facially they are more like a *Gitus*.

The two sub-species differ somewhat in their brain types. *T. fatuselessgitus'* brain is only slightly larger than *Drummus* and reacts in a similar way, only doing some work when kicked hard etc. *T. fullofthemselvsus*, has a larger cerebral cortex, although the bulk of the brain is identical to *T. fatuselessgitus*.

HABITS

Naturally lazy, these creatures will only ever get out of bed to go and sign on and collect their benefit money. *T. fatuselessgitus* is never permanently employed and once a week will struggle out of bed to see if he can get on a tour. *T. fullofthemselvsus* are much more likely to have a permanent job, the difficulty of which will always be grossly exaggerated when describing what they do to anyone not in the know.

FOOD

All species of *Technopissartisae* eat in a similar way. They begin each meal with two pints of lager. The meal itself is always drenched in tomato or brown sauce - even successful *Technopissartisae* will give themselves away in an expensive restaurant. They like fried food, curries and iced buns. They are addicted to nicotine at birth and by the time they're six years old they're on 40 a day. Many will add illegal substances to their cigarettes once they're pushing 80 a day or more. This they believe, is like 'cutting down' a bit.

BREEDING

Technopissartisae always believe that one day they'll actually get to mate with a big star. This is because they are seriously deluded. However, by the time they are thinking about sex, they are completely pissed and anyone will do. On tour (which is the only time they're fertile), this means mating with the catering girls and make-up artists. As these are actually (and unknown to *Technopissartisae*) the females of the species the breed is kept pure to look after the next generation of *musica*.

WHERE IT IS FOUND

One of the most adaptable creatures *Technopissartisae* can live and sleep almost anywhere. They can live, eat, sleep, mate and go to the toilet in an area less than 2m^2. This makes them cheap to employ when on tour as they are usually quite happy sleeping and doing everything in their coach seat area.

T. fullofthemselvsus is more of a pain in the arse. He's so full of it because he's qualified (ooooooh), that he won't sleep anywhere near *T. fatuselessgitus*. He insists on hotels and eating at a table just as if he was a normal species.

Still, we'd be lost without them - wouldn't we?

ORIGIN

Bullshitus, like *Overpaedus* can exert massive influence and power over other species. Always the result of cross-breeding between either *Ivorytinklus* and *Overpaedus* or *Vocalis* and *Overpaedus*. This gives us our two sub-species of *Bullshitus intelectulus* and *Bullshitus hasntacluus*.

Bullshitus intelectulus can sometimes be a positive force for *musica* species but all too often the *Overpaedus* blood in them is too strong and they can only think in dollars. *Bullshitus hasntacluus* on the other hand is a menace that in an ideal world would be hacked to death by a disgruntled *vocalis*. More often than not though they just end up being shagged by *vocalis* (usually *bimbosexus*), which is just not fair.

SIZE and GENERAL ANATOMY

Easily recognisable and immediately distinguishable from *Overpaedus* because they're only five feet tall. They have luke warm blood and unlike *Overpaedus* have exotic perms rather than close cropped hair.

HABITS

Always busy (they reckon) *Bullshitus* is believed to spend at least 14 hours a day working. Actually this is a myth. They are always at the studio for 14 hours or more but most of this time is spent on the phone or shagging the brains out of a young naive *Vocalis bimbosexus* or *Screechus tooprettytobeseriousae*. Only about 2 hours are spent actually producing, or more accurately telling other people what they want and then leaving the control room to get some more sex.

FOOD

Expensive and prepared by someone else with cocaine for afters.

BREEDING

All the time. There is no such thing as a pure bred *Bullshitus* - they occur naturally through cross-breeding as mentioned earlier in 'ORIGIN'.

WHERE IT IS FOUND

Mock tutor mansions and hideous grandiose penthouses. Just look for excessive security systems.

ORIGIN

Overpaedus have existed long before the invention of records and CDs. Like all of the *submusica* species they evolved wherever there were pockets of evolving *musica*. Very closely related to *Hangersonus insidius* and *fleecus* - indeed they almost certainly have evolved from cross-breeding between the two most ancient breeds of *Hangersonus*.

SIZE and GENERAL ANATOMY

Generally unnecessarily tall, these creatures have lost most of the visible characteristics of their original ancestors. However, their blood is still cold and their feet are still webbed. One reason they're so dangerous for other species is because their outward appearance is so normal. In fact they have an almost identical brain to *Hangersonus insidius* and *fleecus*.

HABITS

During the day they must be on the phone at least 90% of their time and in a meeting at all other times. The most skilled can juggle seven calls at the same time. At night they descend on trendy restaurants and then annoy the entire clientele by spending the entire evening on their mobile phones. They can maintain this lifestyle for as long as they have a huge expense account.

FOOD

Any food so long as it's expensive and prepared by someone else. If they ever had to feed themselves they'd starve to death. Cocaine is also an essential part of their diet.

BREEDING

They spend much of their time trying it on with *Vocalis*. They rarely have time for other species but usually *vocalis* are not interested in them so eventually they have to breed with their own kind, which has kept the breed pure.

WHERE IT IS FOUND

They need to keep cool in order to think that they are cool. Originally cave dwellers (albeit designer caves) they now live in expensive loft conversions in large cities. During the day they can only exist in air conditioned luxury. A failed *Overpaedus* will not live long once forced to walk rather than get a cab or limo.

ublished by R & C Gregory Publishing Ltd

ISBN 1-901690-15-6

ISBN 1-901690-11-3

Learn Guitar From Beginner To Your 1st Band, by John A. MacLachlan. This book comes with a free CD produced to make you feel part of the band from day 1.

A Step By Step Guide To Everything You Need To Know About Being A Guitar Player, by John A. MacLachlan. This tutor book packs a punch of information to get you started in guitar playing.

for *Basso simplex & complex*

The Pro' Series

Clive Gregory's

FOUNDATION COURSE

for

BASS GUITAR

ISBN 1-901690-16-4

ISBN 1-901690-09-1

ISBN 1-901690-20-2

Learn Bass From Beginner To Your 1st Band, by Clive Gregory. This book comes with a free CD produced to make you feel part of the band from day 1.

A Great Way To Learn Bass, by Clive Gregory. This tutor book packs a punch of information to get you started in bass playing.

Clive Gregory's Foundation Course For Bass Guitar. This book is the probably the most thorough tutor book for beginners to intermediate students.

for *Drummus*

ISBN 1-901690-13-X

A Step By Step Guide To Everything You Need To Know About Being A Drummer, by Neil Martin. This tutor book packs a punch of information to get you started in drumming.

for *Ivorytinklus*

ISBN 1-901690-12-1

A Step By Step Guide To Everything You Need To Know About Being A Keyboard Player, by Geoff Ellwood. This tutor book packs a punch of information to get you started in keyboard playing.

for *Blowjobus saxus*

ISBN 1-901690-14-8

A Step By Step Guide To Everything You Need To Know About Being A Sax Player, by David 'Baps' Baptiste. This tutor book packs a punch of information to get you started in sax playing.